FOR ORGANS, PIANOS & ELECTRONIC KEYBOARDS

E-Z PLAY® TODAY

133

Carole King

T0081997

Cover photo © 2007 by Elissa Kline

ISBN 978-1-4584-0307-0

HAL•LEONARD®
CORPORATION

7777 W. BLUEMOUND RD. P.O. BOX 13819 MILWAUKEE, WI 53213

In Australia Contact:
Hal Leonard Australia Pty. Ltd.
4 Lentara Court
Cheltenham, Victoria, 3192 Australia
Email: ausadmin@halleonard.com.au

For all works contained herein:
Unauthorized copying, arranging, adapting, recording, Internet posting, public performance,
or other distribution of the printed music in this publication is an infringement of copyright.
Infringers are liable under the law.

E-Z Play® Today Music Notation © 1975 by HAL LEONARD CORPORATION
E-Z PLAY and EASY ELECTRONIC KEYBOARD MUSIC are registered trademarks of HAL LEONARD CORPORATION.

Visit Hal Leonard Online at
www.halleonard.com

Beautiful

Registration 4
Rhythm: 8-Beat or Rock

Words and Music by
Carole King

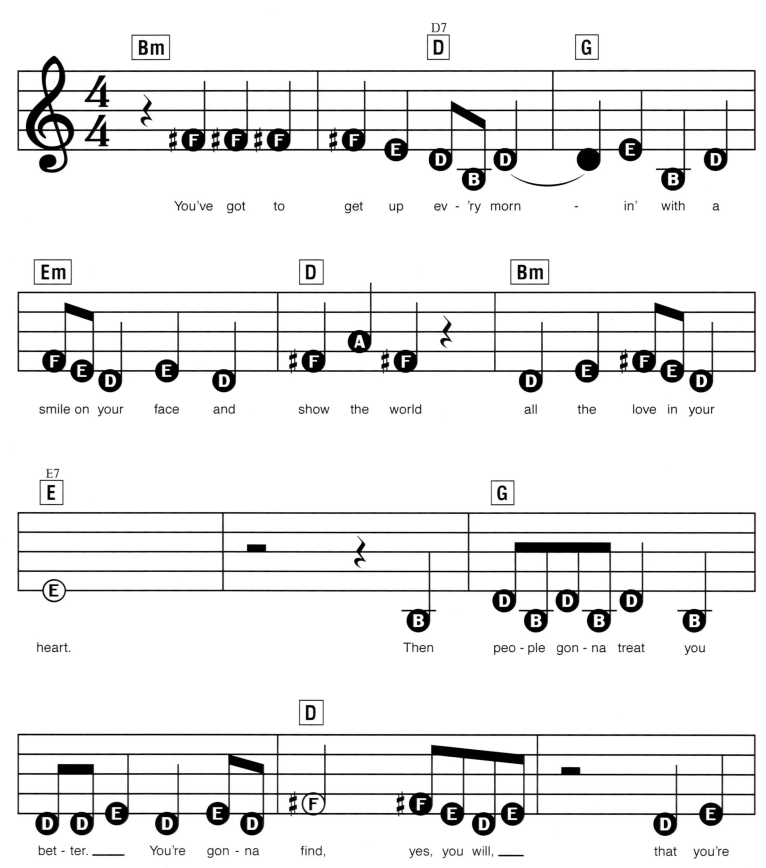

© 1971 (Renewed 1999) COLGEMS-EMI MUSIC INC.
All Rights Reserved   International Copyright Secured   Used by Permission

5

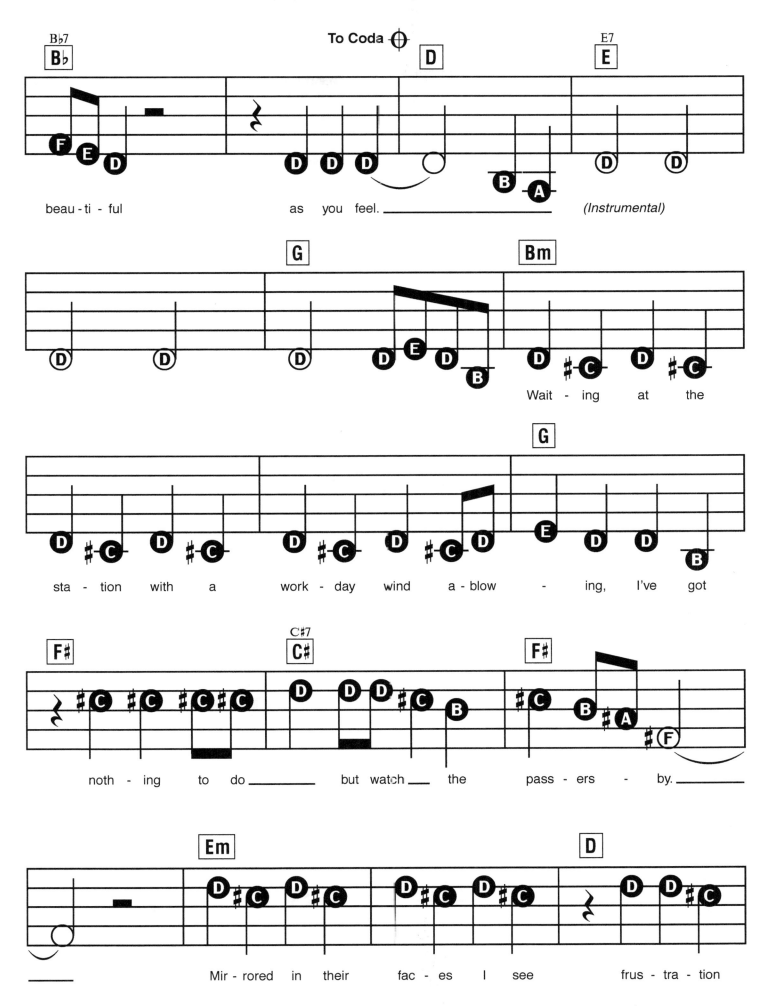

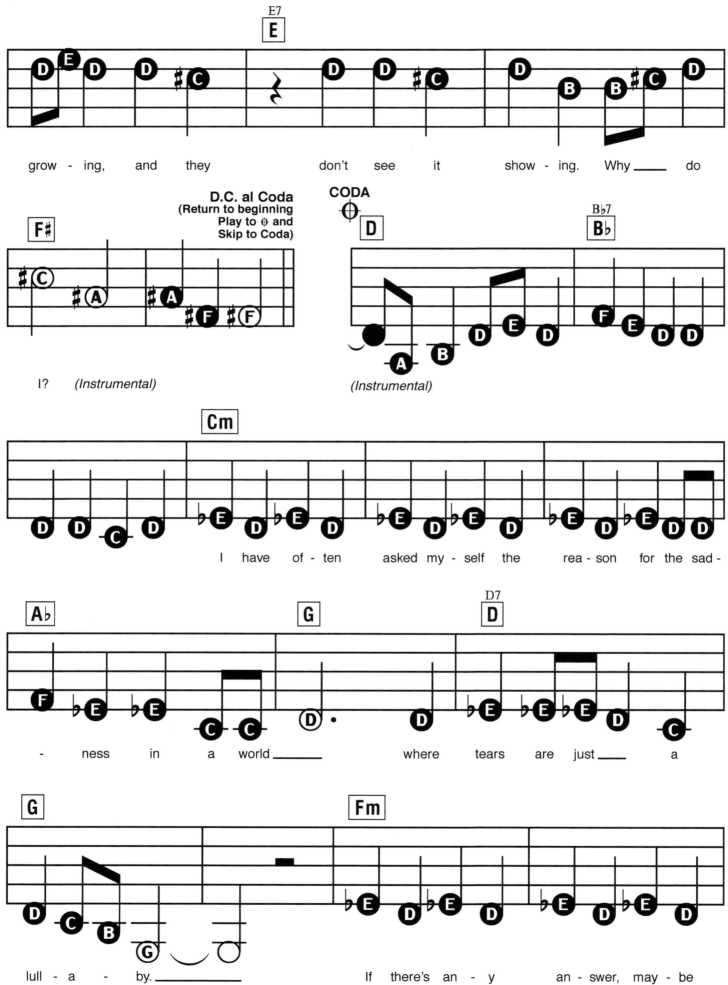

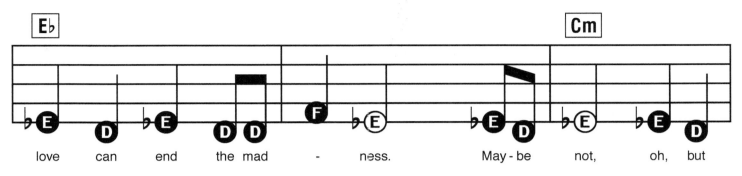

love can end the mad - ness. May - be not, oh, but

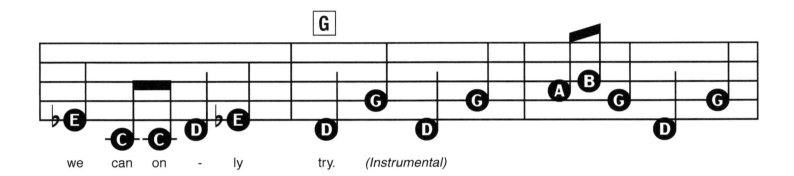

we can on - ly try. *(Instrumental)*

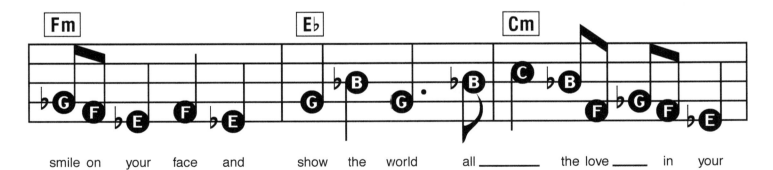

You've got to get up ev - 'ry morn - in' with a

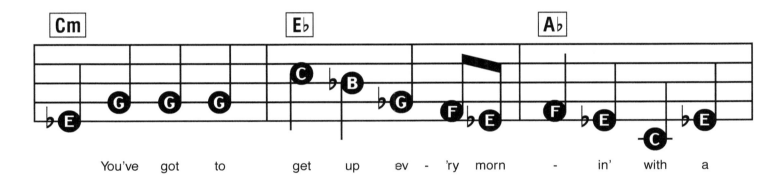

smile on your face and show the world all _____ the love _____ in your

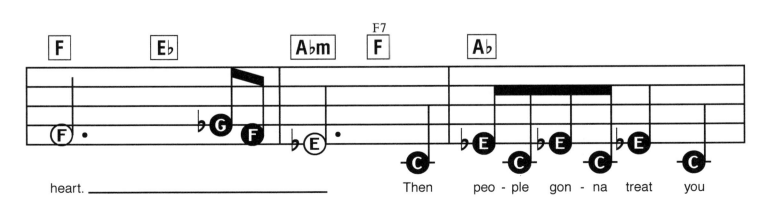

heart. _____ Then peo - ple gon - na treat you

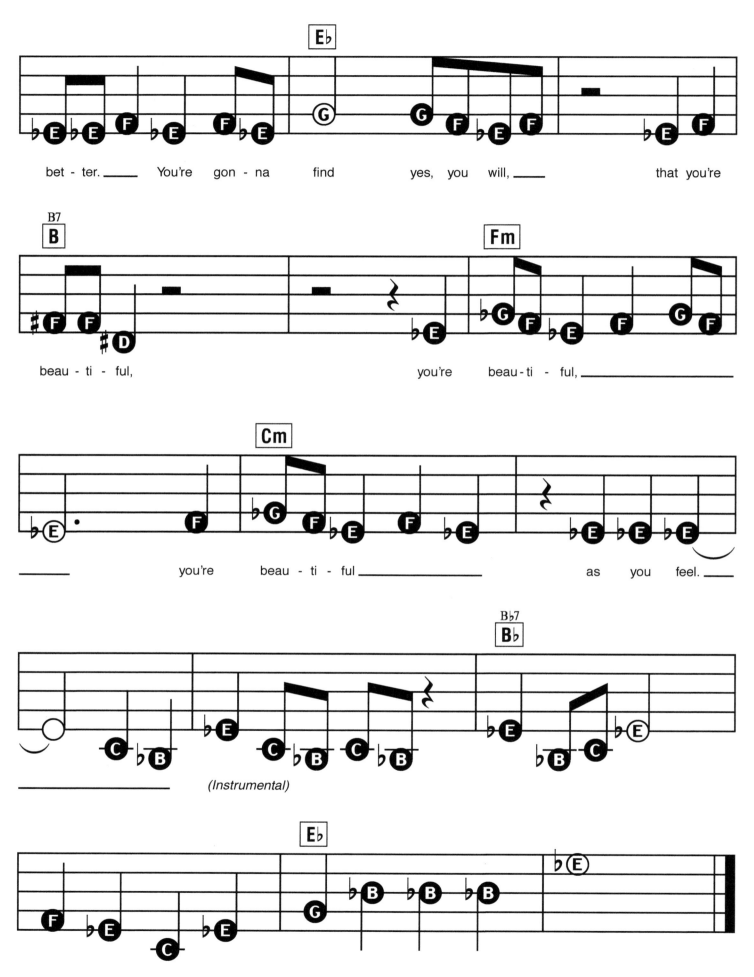

Chains

Registration 2
Rhythm: Rock or Shuffle

Words and Music by Gerry Goffin
and Carole King

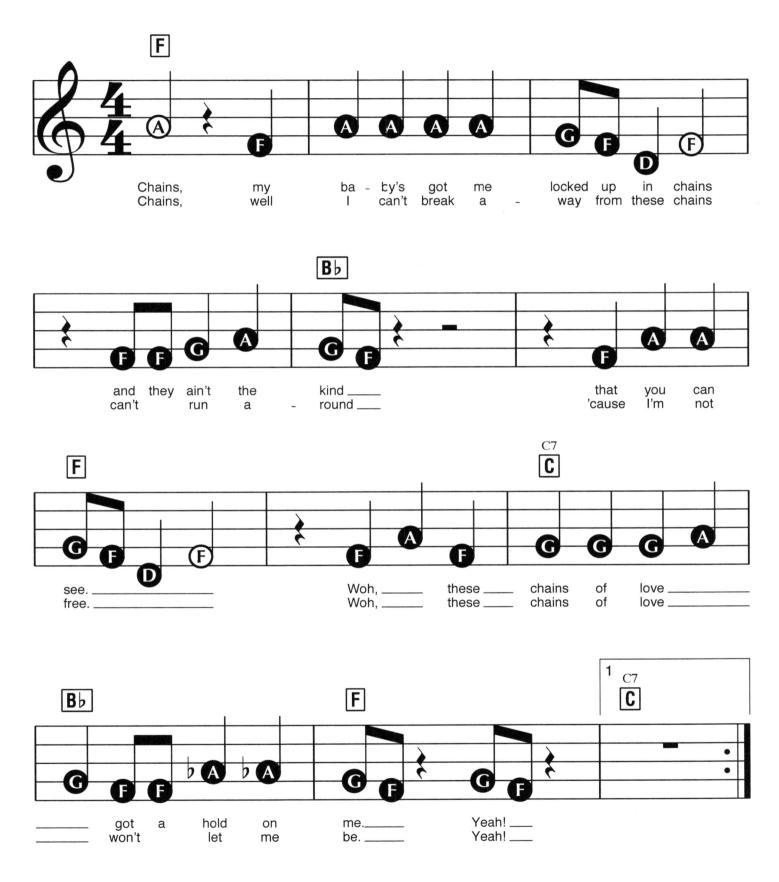

Chains, my ba-by's got me locked up in chains
Chains, well I can't break a - way from these chains

and they ain't the kind ____ that you can
can't run a - round ____ 'cause I'm not

see. ____ Woh, ____ these ____ chains of love ____
free. ____ Woh, ____ these ____ chains of love ____

____ got a hold on me. ____ Yeah! ____
____ won't let me be. ____ Yeah! ____

© 1962 (Renewed 1990) SCREEN GEMS-EMI MUSIC INC.
All Rights Reserved   International Copyright Secured   Used by Permission

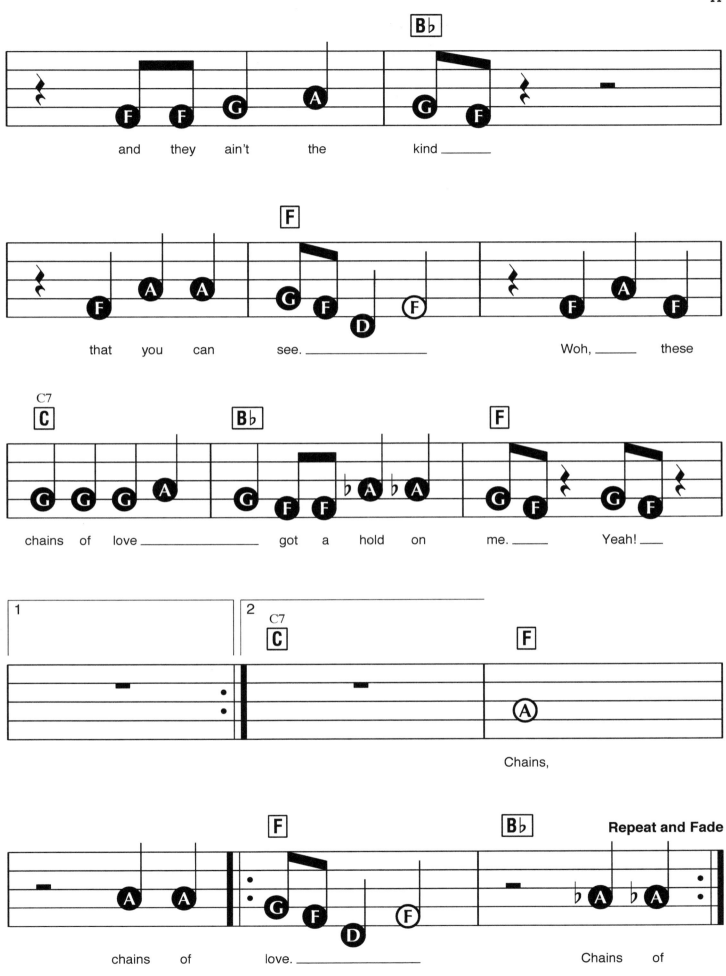

Home Again

Registration 8
Rhythm: 8-Beat or Rock

Words and Music by
Carole King

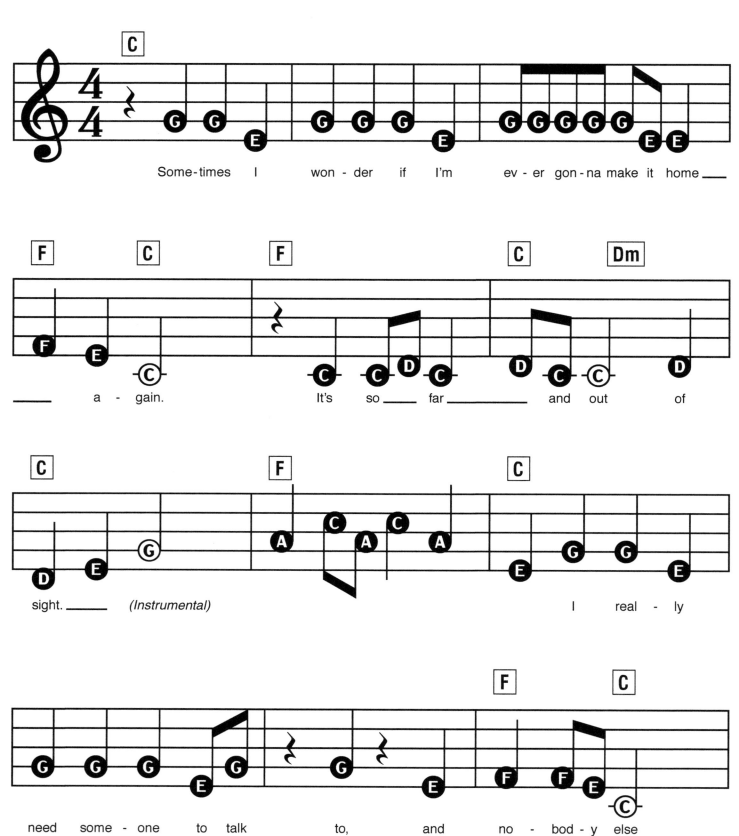

© 1971 (Renewed 1999) COLGEMS-EMI MUSIC INC.
All Rights Reserved   International Copyright Secured   Used by Permission

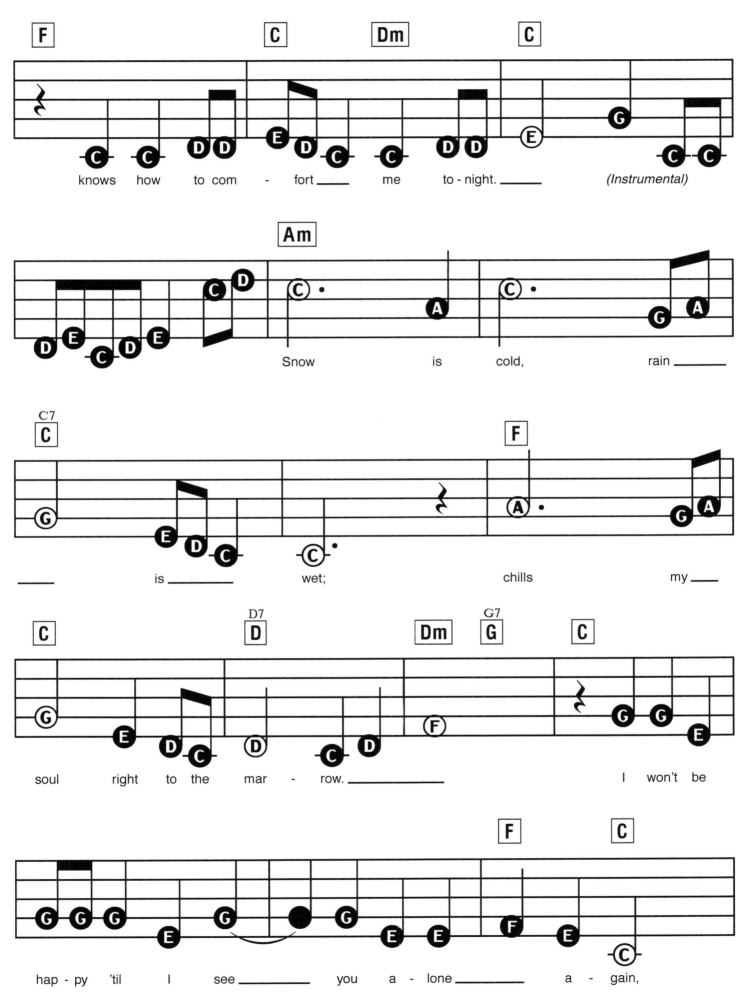

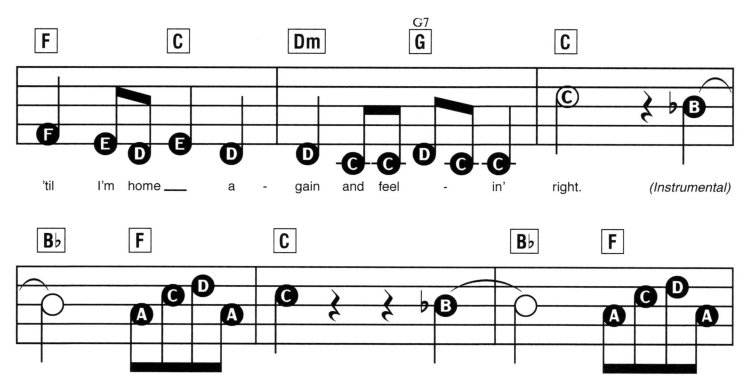

'til I'm home ___ a - gain and feel - in' right.   *(Instrumental)*

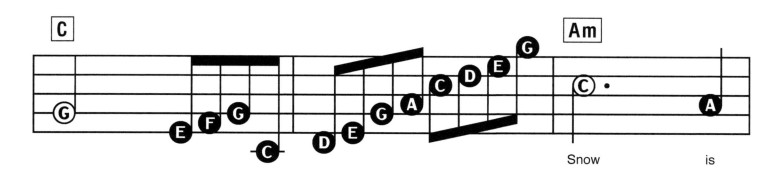

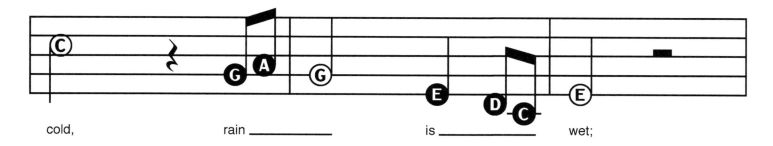

Snow   is

cold,   rain _____ is _____ wet;

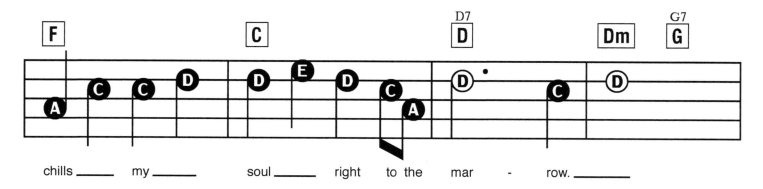

chills ___ my ___ soul ___ right to the mar - row. ___

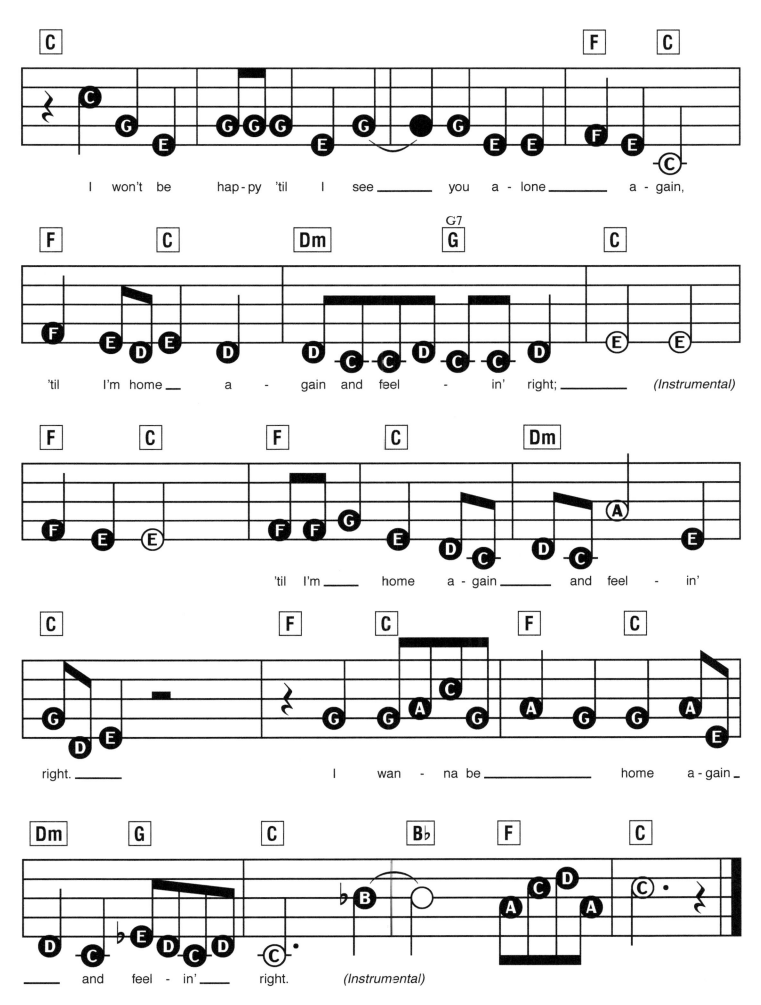

I Feel the Earth Move

Registration 4
Rhythm: Rock

Words and Music by
Carole King

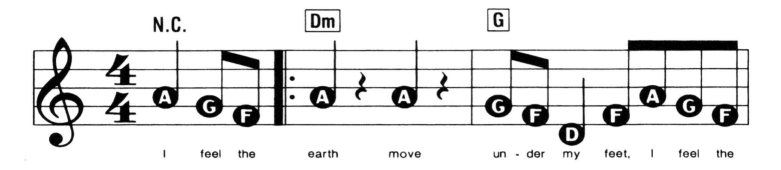

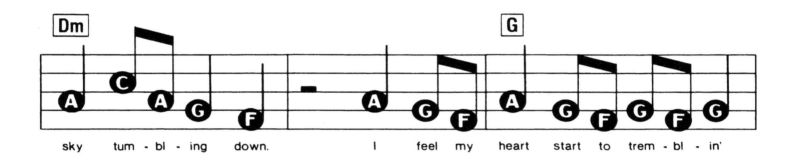

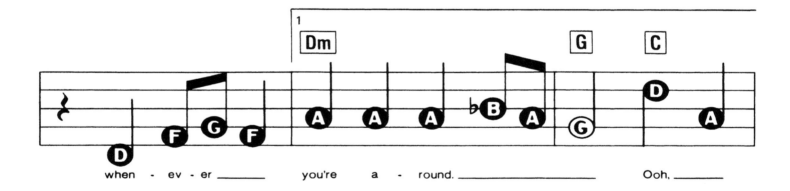

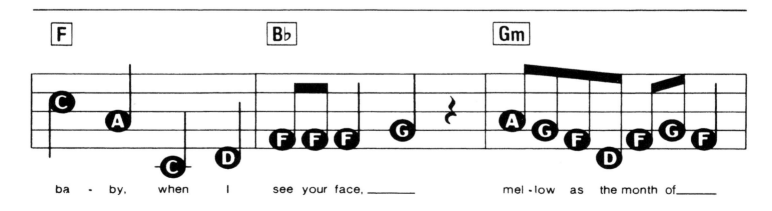

© 1971 (Renewed 1999) COLGEMS-EMI MUSIC INC.
All Rights Reserved   International Copyright Secured   Used by Permission

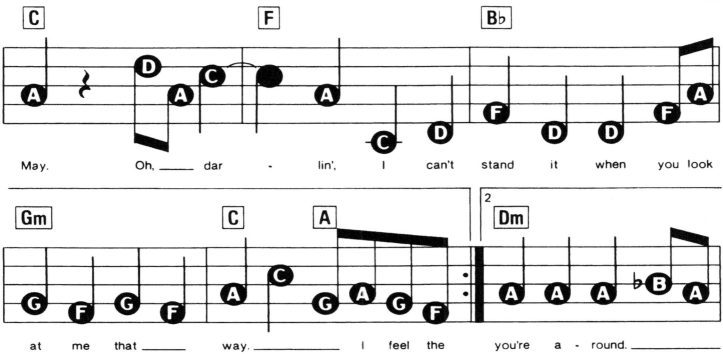

May. Oh, ____ dar - lin', I can't stand it when you look

at me that ____ way. ____ I feel the you're a - round. ____

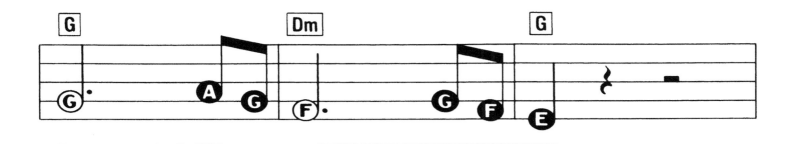

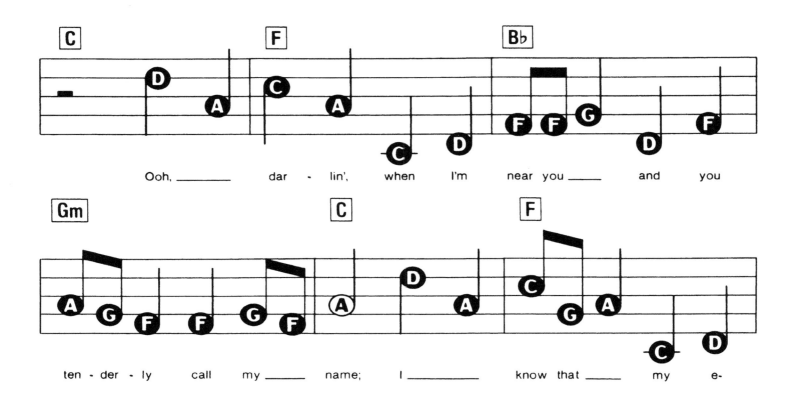

Ooh, ____ dar - lin', when I'm near you ____ and you

ten - der - ly call my ____ name; I ____ know that ____ my e-

18

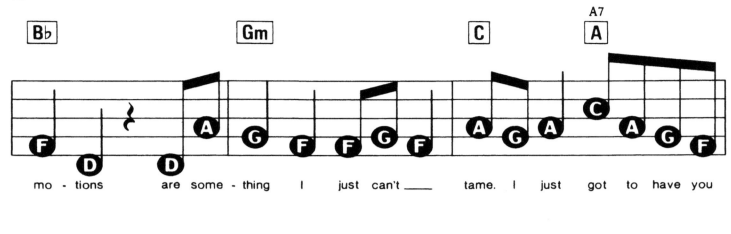

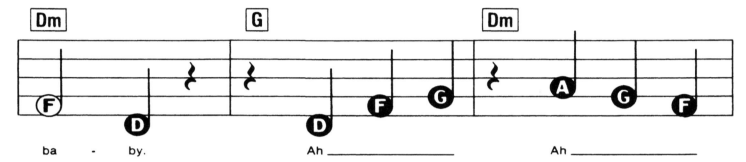

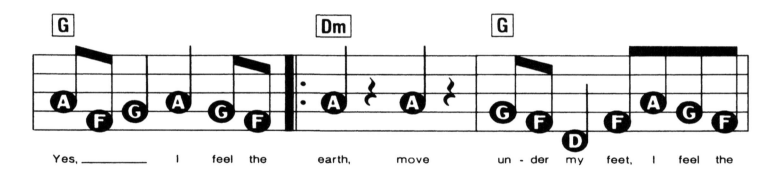

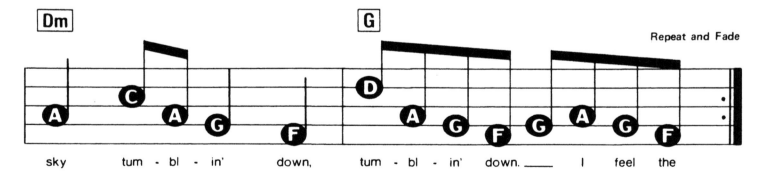

Additional Lyrics

I just lose control down to my very soul,
I get hot and cold all over, all over, all over.

Jazzman

Registration 7
Rhythm: Rock

Words and Music by Carole King
and David Palmer

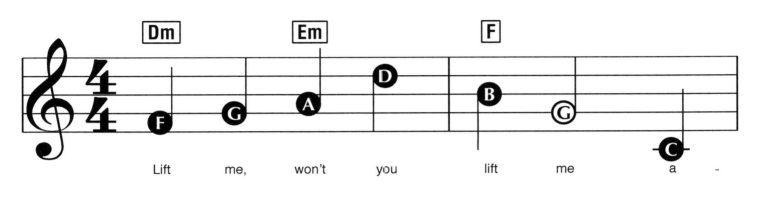

Lift me, won't you lift me a-

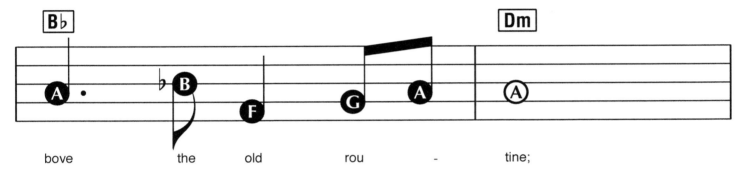

bove the old rou - tine;

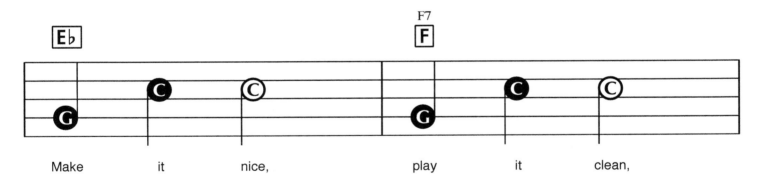

Make it nice, play it clean,

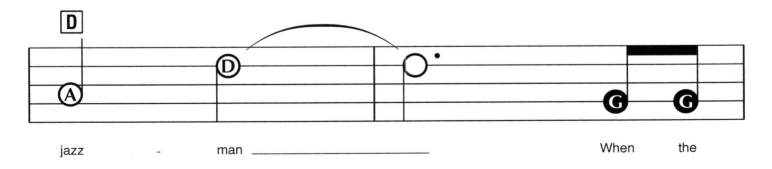

jazz - man _____ When the

© 1974 (Renewed 2002) COLGEMS-EMI MUSIC INC. and ELORAC MUSIC, INC.
All Rights Controlled and Administered by COLGEMS-EMI MUSIC INC.
All Rights Reserved International Copyright Secured Used by Permission

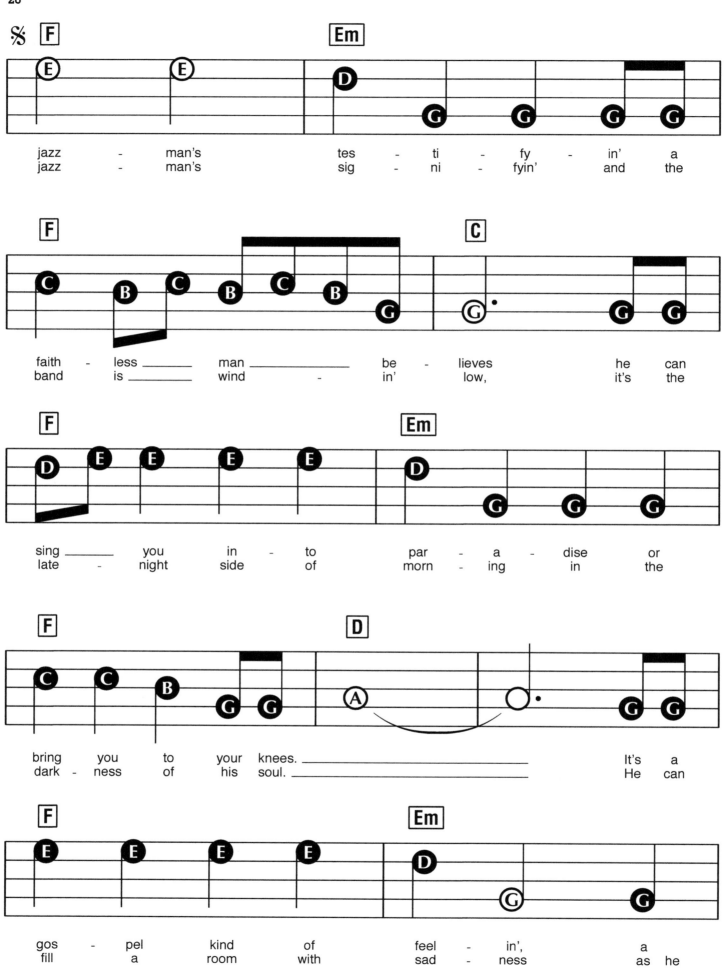

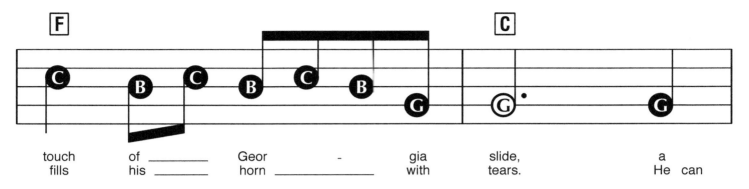

touch   of _____   Geor - gia   slide,   a
fills   his _____   horn _____   with   tears.   He   can

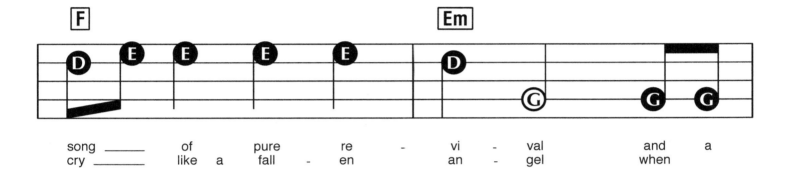

song _____   of   pure   re - vi - val   and   a
cry _____   like   a   fall - en   an - gel   when

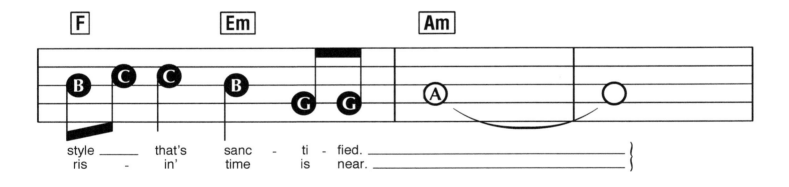

style _____   that's   sanc - ti - fied. _____
ris - in'   time   is   near. _____

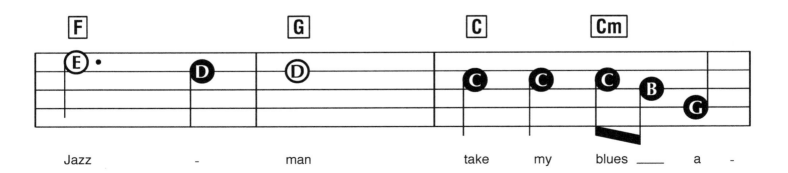

Jazz -   man   take   my   blues ___   a -

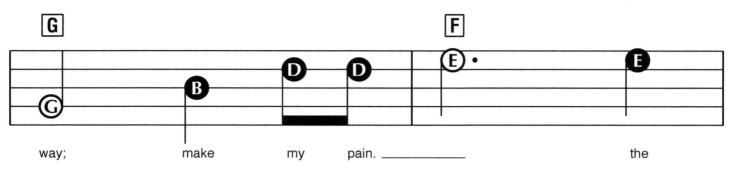

way; make my pain. _____ the

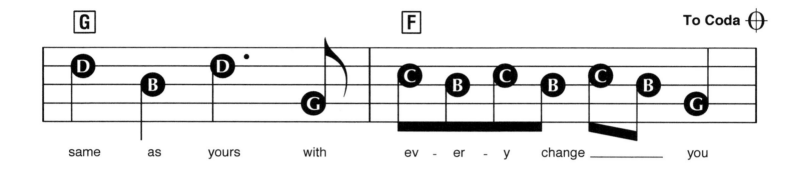

To Coda ⊕

same as yours with ev - er - y change _____ you

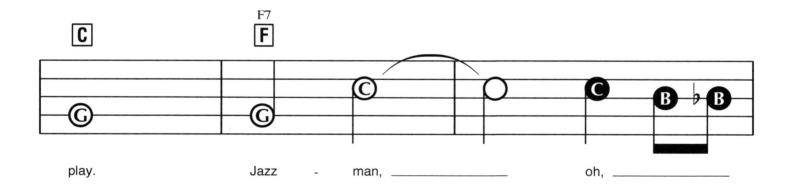

play. Jazz - man, _____ oh, _____

D.S. al Coda
(Return to 𝄋
Play to ⊕ and
Skip to Coda)

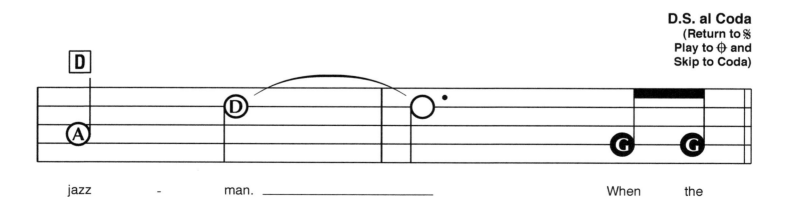

jazz - man. _____ When the

CODA

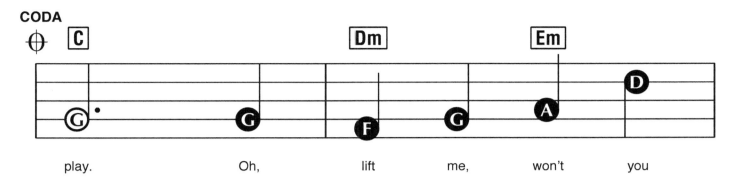

play.   Oh,   lift   me,   won't   you

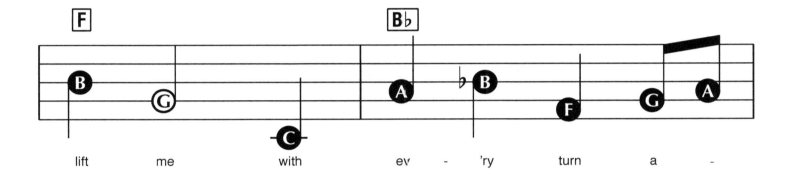

lift   me   with   ev - 'ry   turn   a -

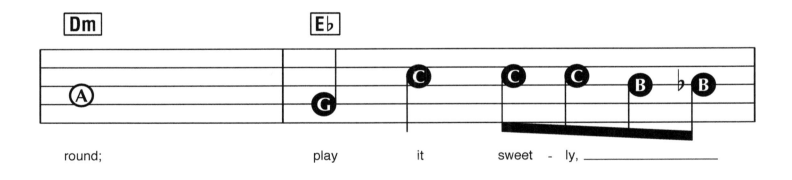

round;   play   it   sweet - ly, _____

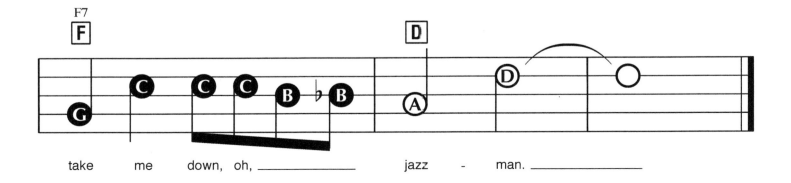

take   me   down,   oh, _____   jazz - man. _____

It's Too Late

Registration 8
Rhythm: 8-Beat or Rock

Words and Music by Carole King
and Toni Stern

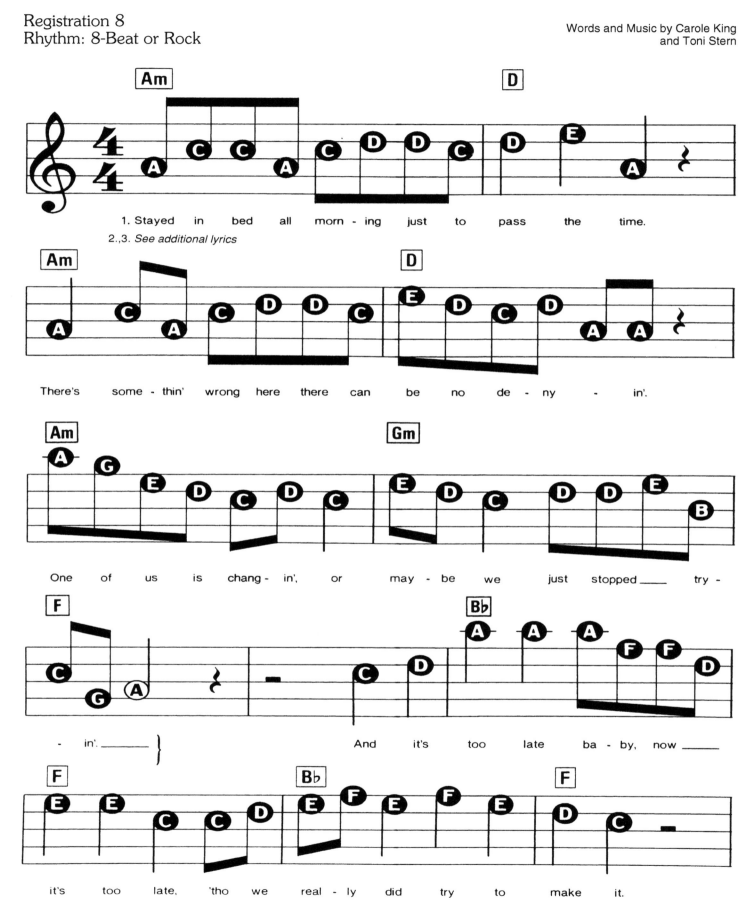

© 1971 (Renewed 1999) COLGEMS-EMI MUSIC INC.
All Rights Reserved International Copyright Secured Used by Permission

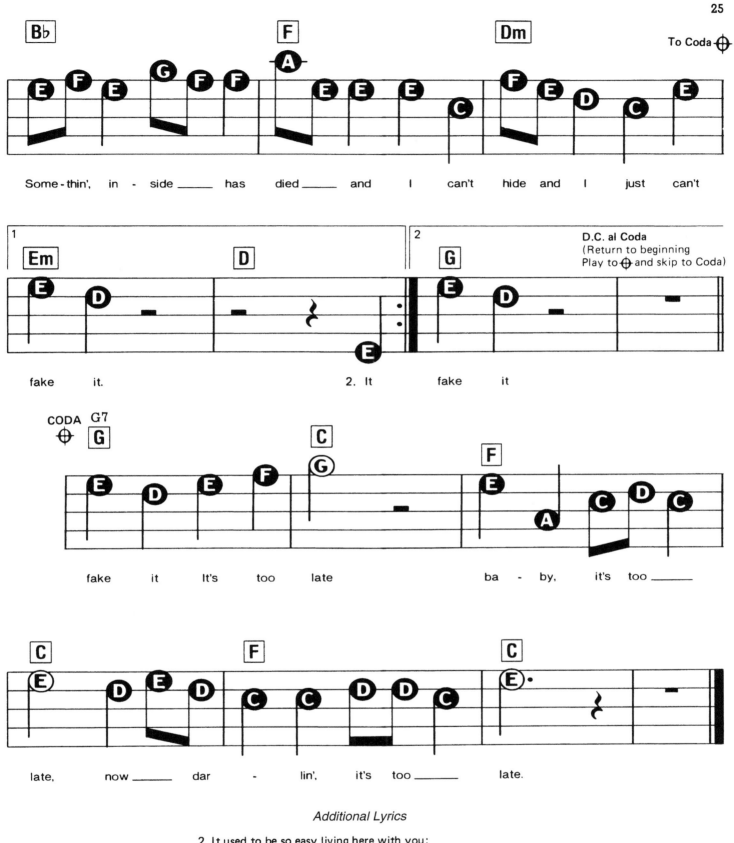

Additional Lyrics

2. It used to be so easy living here with you;
You were light and breezy and
I knew just what to do.
Now you look so unhappy and I feel like a fool.

3. There'll be good times again for me and you;
But we just can't stay together,
Don't you feel it too?
Still I'm glad for what we had and how I once loved you.

The Loco-Motion

Registration 4
Rhythm: Rock

Words and Music by Gerry Goffin
and Carole King

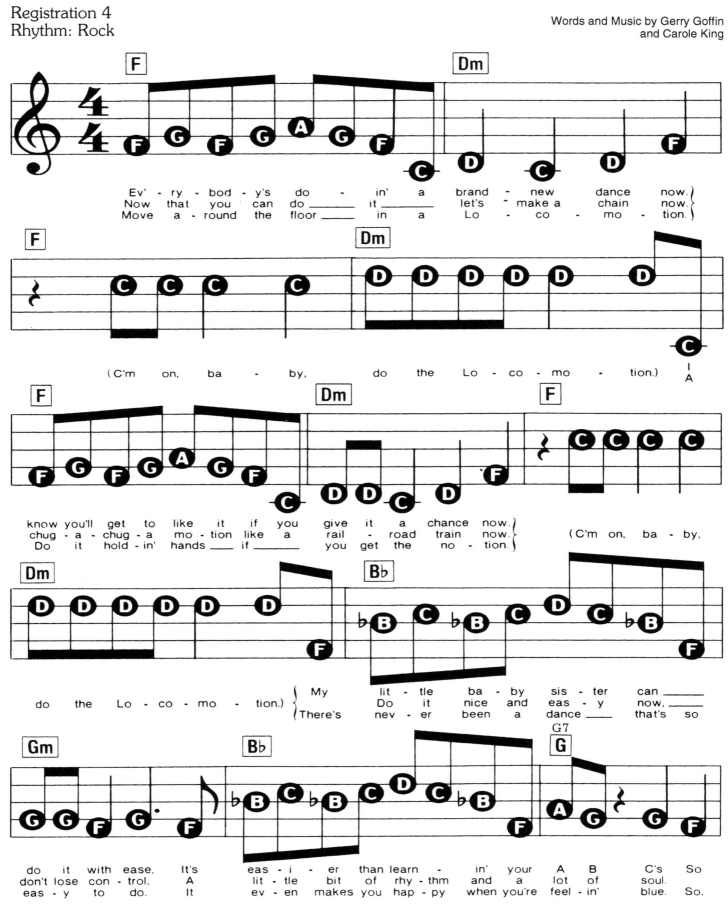

© 1962 (Renewed 1990) SCREEN GEMS-EMI MUSIC INC.
All Rights Reserved   International Copyright Secured   Used by Permission

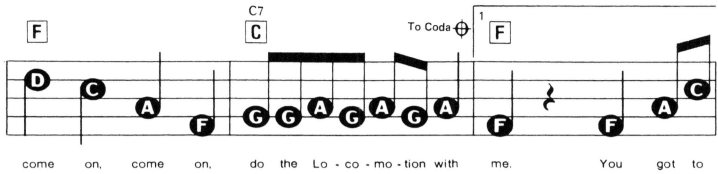

come on, come on, do the Lo - co - mo - tion with me. You got to

swing your hips now, Come on, ba - by, jump up, jump

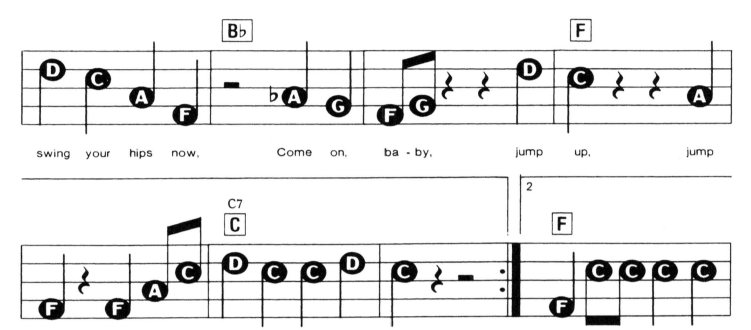

back; Oh well, I think you got the knack. me. (C'm-on, ba - by,

D.C. al Coda
(Return to beginning
Play to ⊕ and skip
to Coda)

CODA
⊕

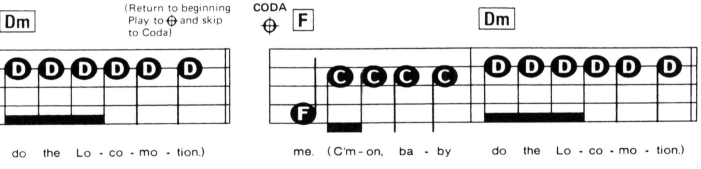

do the Lo - co - mo - tion.) me. (C'm - on, ba - by do the Lo - co - mo - tion.)

Repeat and Fade

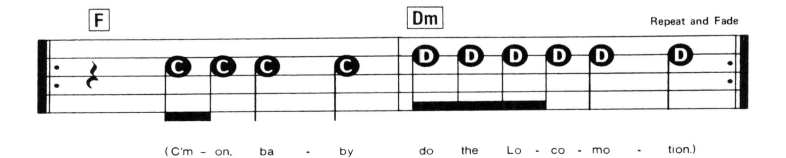

(C'm - on, ba - by do the Lo - co - mo - tion.)

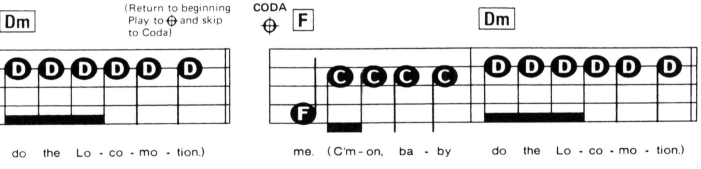

(You Make Me Feel Like)
A Natural Woman

Registration 7
Rhythm: Waltz or Slow Rock

Words and Music by Gerry Goffin,
Carole King and Jerry Wexler

© 1967 (Renewed 1995) SCREEN GEMS-EMI MUSIC INC.
All Rights Reserved   International Copyright Secured   Used by Permission

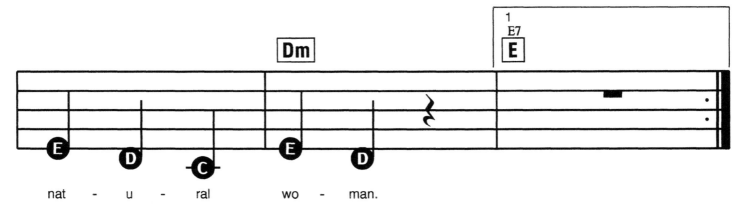

nat - u - ral   wo - man.

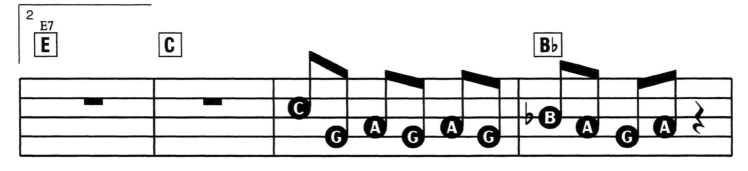

Oh, ___   ba - by what you've   done   to   me! ___

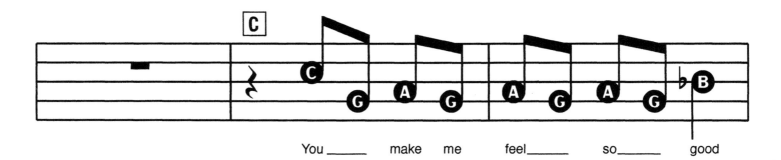

You ___   make   me   feel ___   so ___   good

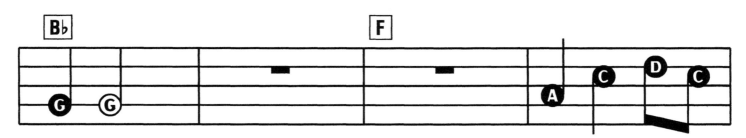

in - side.   And   I   just ___

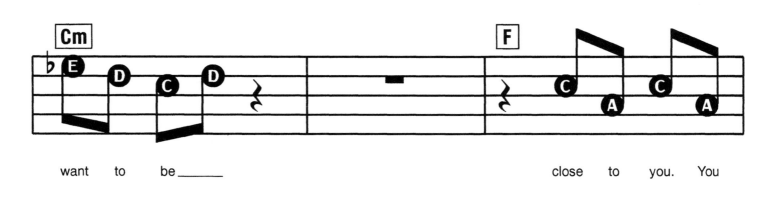

want   to   be ___   close   to   you.   You

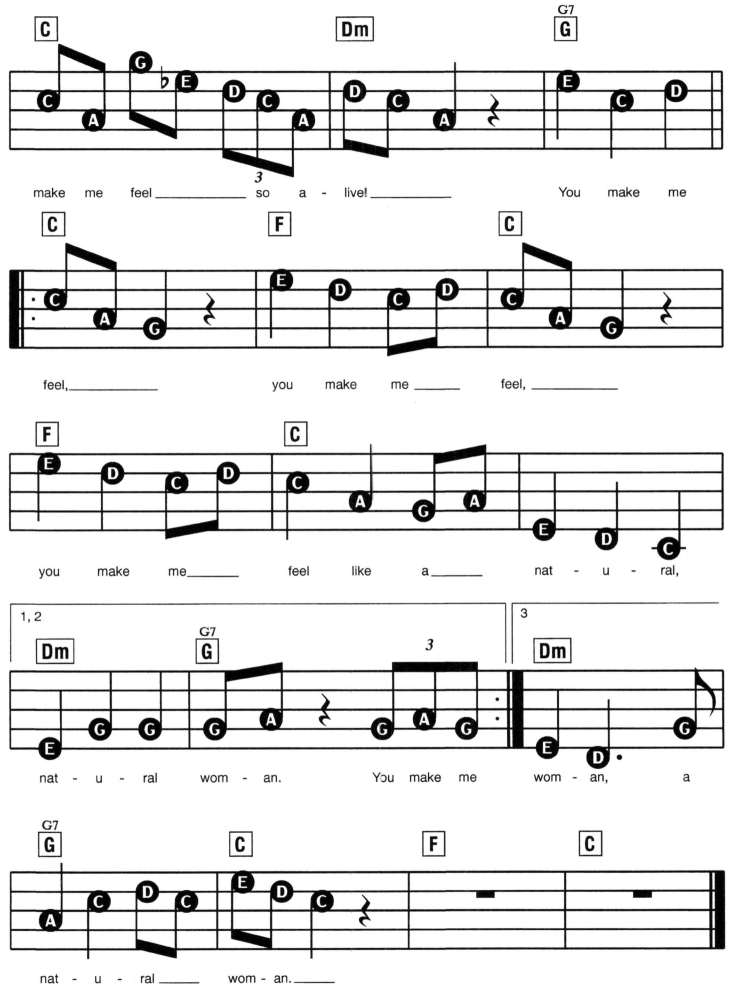

Smackwater Jack

Registration 4
Rhythm: Swing

Words and Music by Gerry Goffin
and Carole King

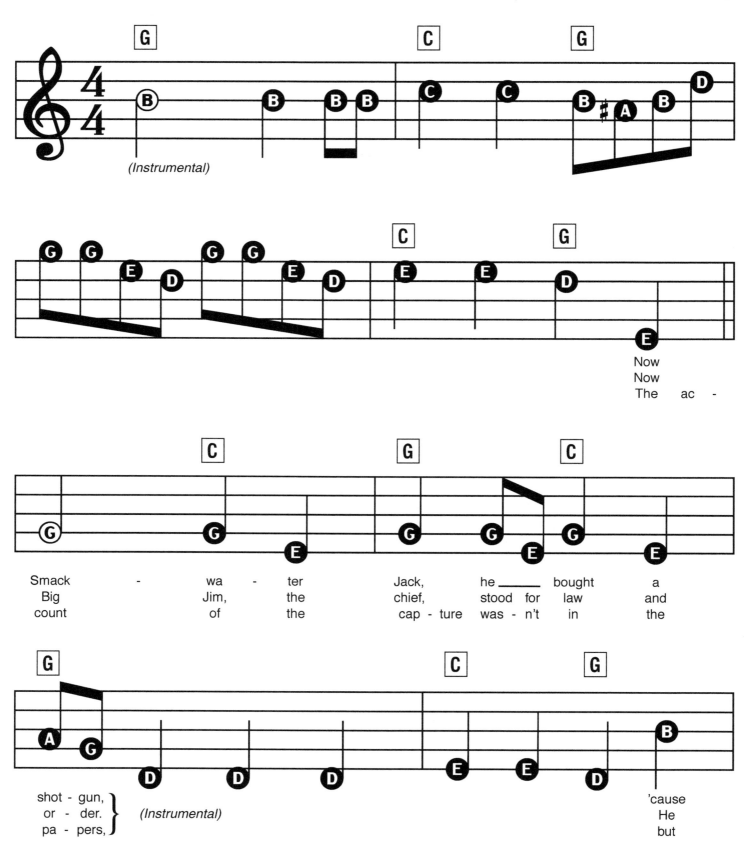

© 1971 (Renewed 1999) SCREEN GEMS-EMI MUSIC INC.
All Rights Reserved   International Copyright Secured   Used by Permission

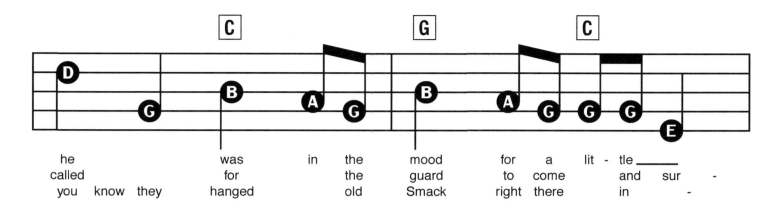

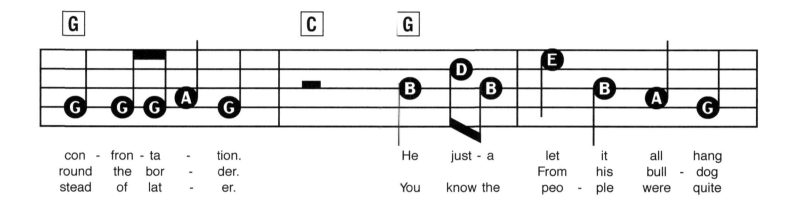

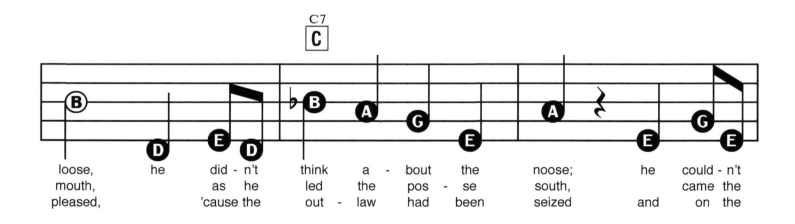

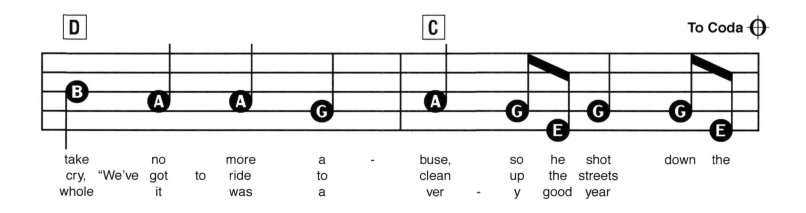

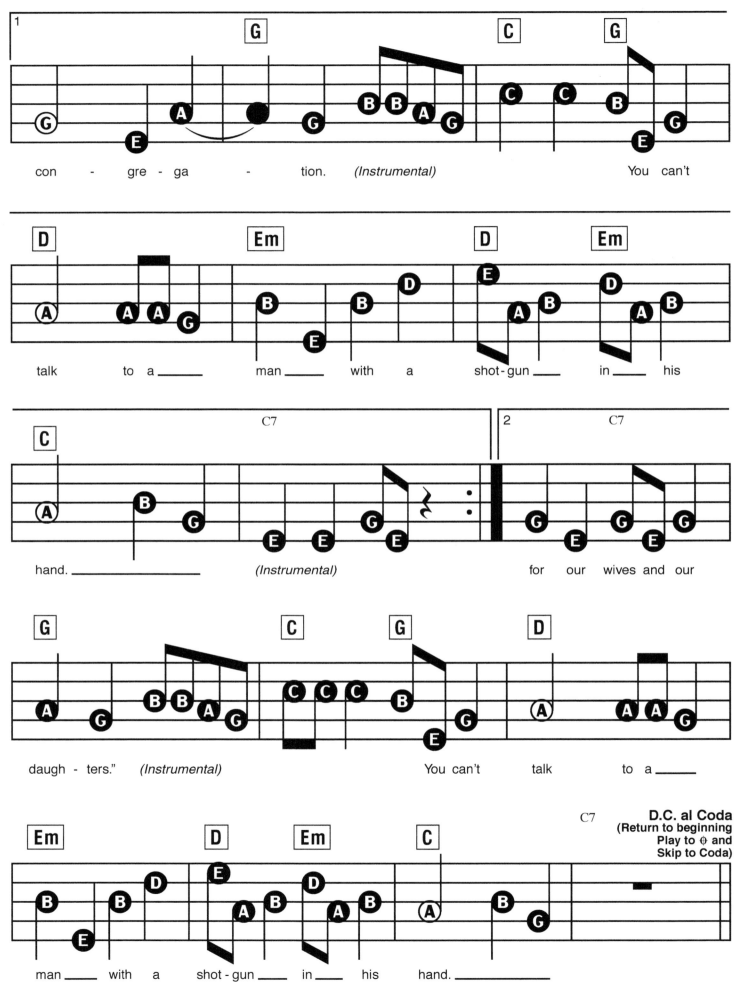

<remixB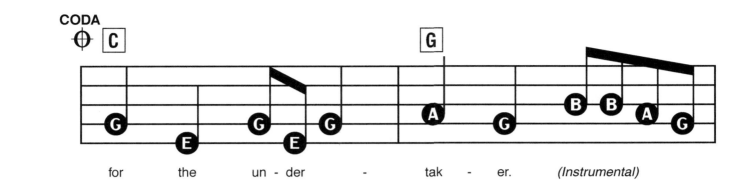

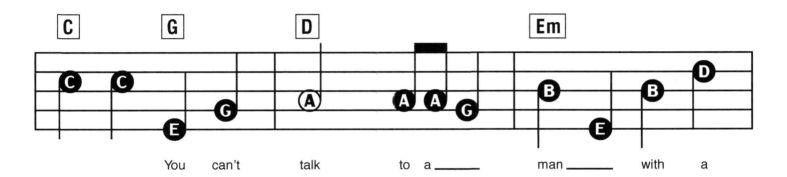

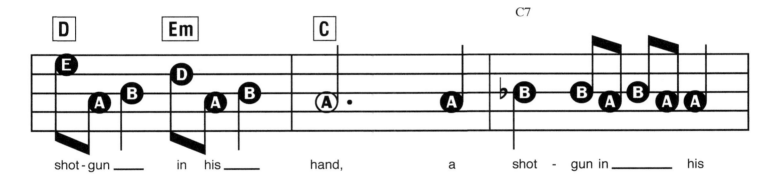

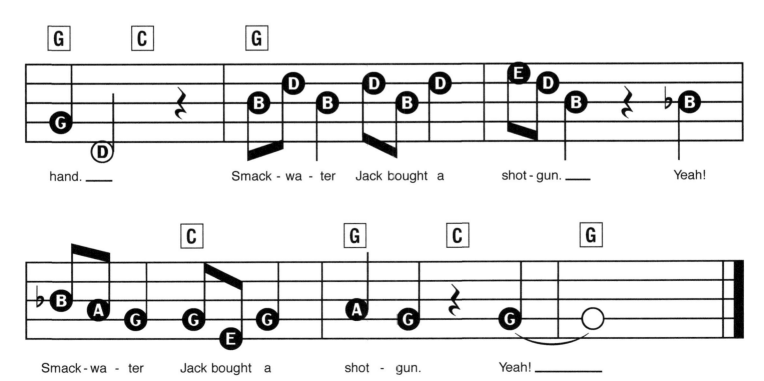

So Far Away

Registration 4
Rhythm: Ballad

Words and Music by
Carole King

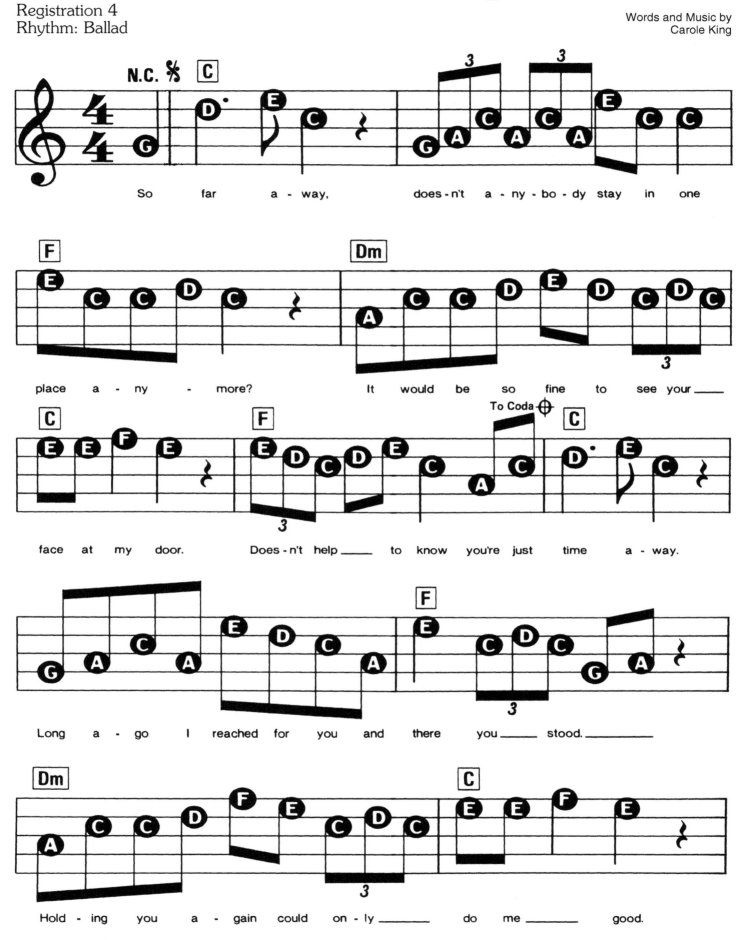

© 1971 (Renewed 1999) COLGEMS-EMI MUSIC INC.
All Rights Reserved International Copyright Secured Used by Permission

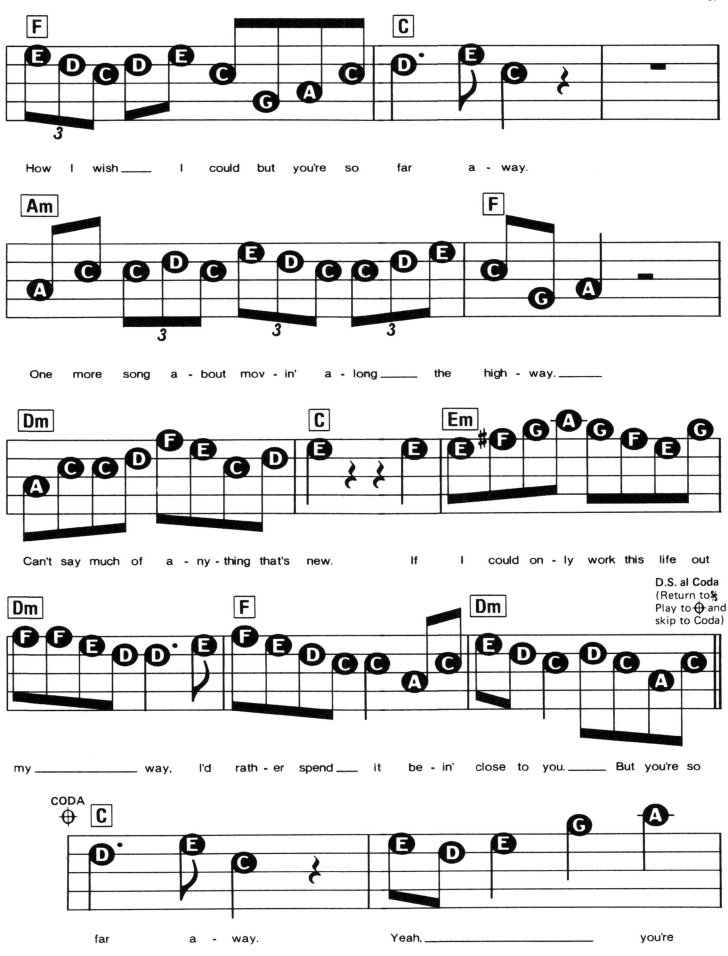

How I wish____ I could but you're so far a - way.

One more song a - bout mov - in' a - long____ the high - way.____

Can't say much of a - ny - thing that's new. If I could on - ly work this life out

D.S. al Coda
(Return to %
Play to ⊕ and
skip to Coda)

my_____ way, I'd rath - er spend____ it be - in' close to you.____ But you're so

CODA

far a - way. Yeah,_____ you're

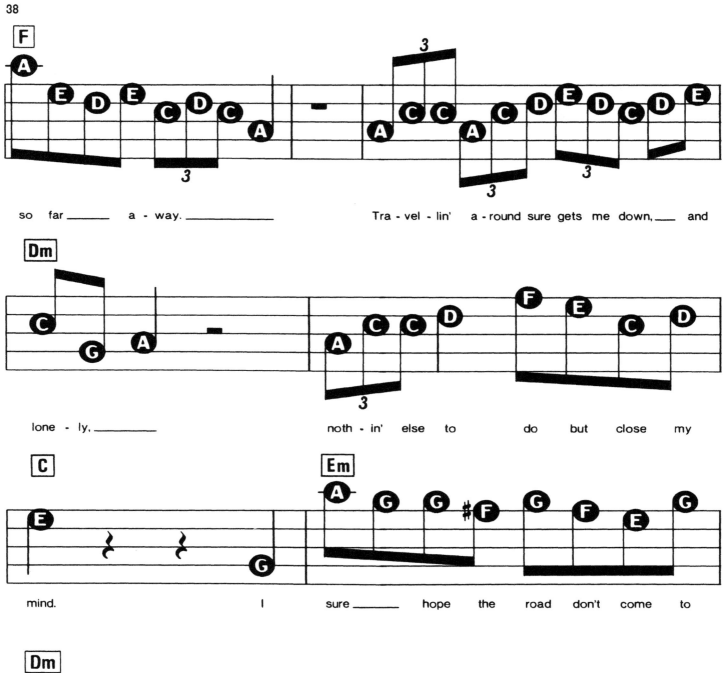

so far _____ a - way. _____ Tra - vel - lin' a - round sure gets me down,___ and

lone - ly, _____ noth - in' else to do but close my

mind. I sure _____ hope the road don't come to

own _____ me; there's so ma - ny dreams_____ I've

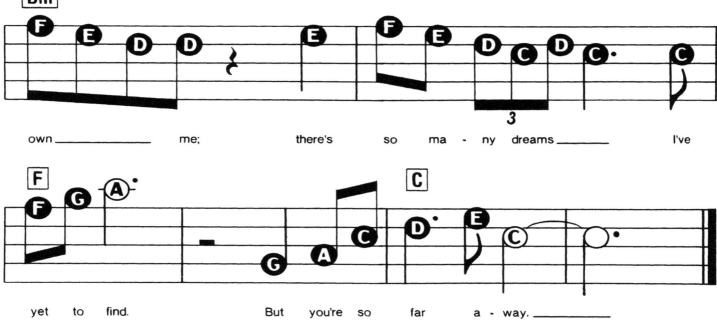

yet to find. But you're so far a - way. _____

Sweet Seasons

Registration 4
Rhythm: 8-Beat or Rock

Words and Music by Carole King
and Toni Stern

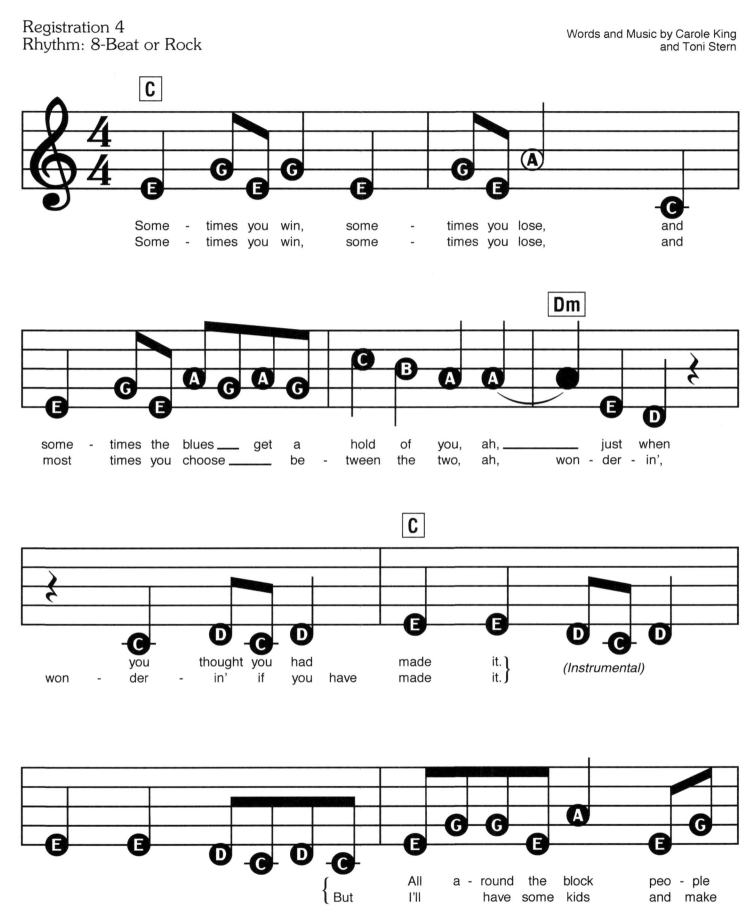

© 1971 (Renewed 1999) COLGEMS-EMI MUSIC INC. and BLUE GUITAR MUSIC
All Rights Controlled and Administered by COLGEMS-EMI MUSIC INC.
All Rights Reserved   International Copyright Secured   Used by Permission

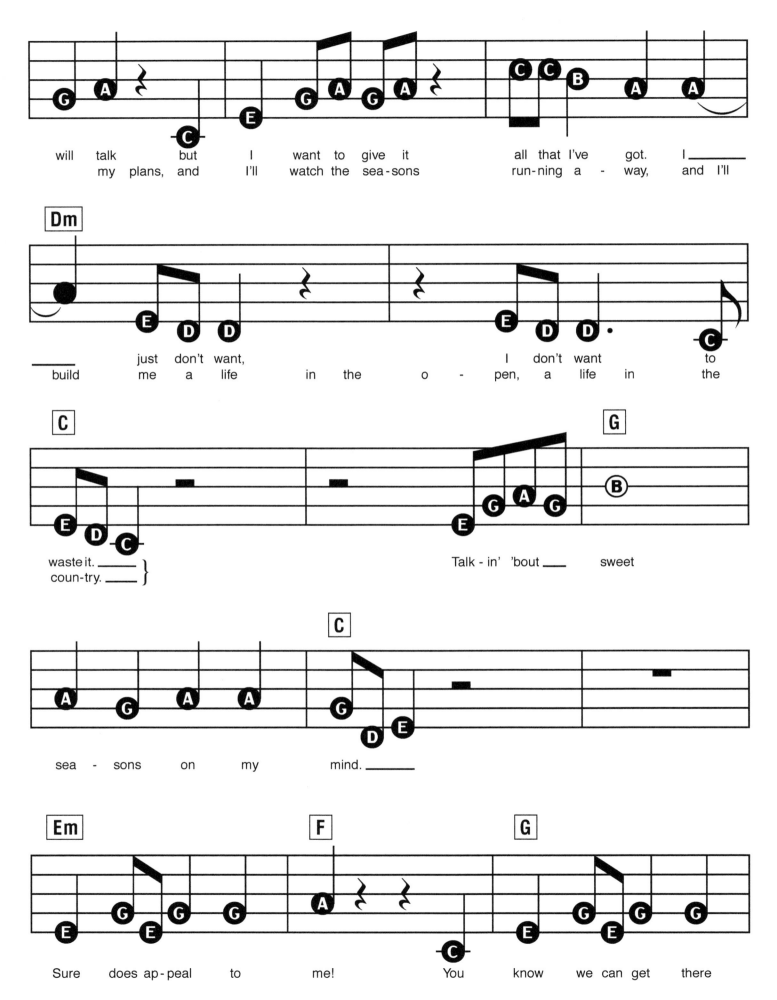

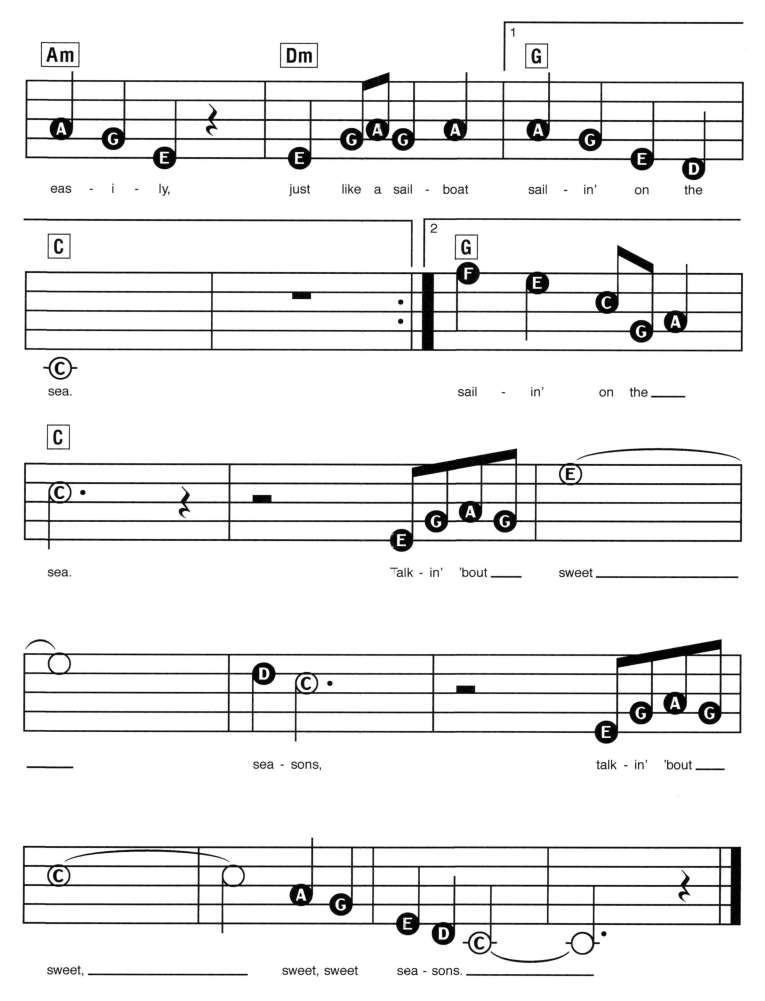

Tapestry

Registration 4
Rhythm: 8-Beat or Rock

Words and Music by
Carole King

My life has been a tap - es - try of
As I watched in sor - row there

rich and roy - al hue. An ev - er - last - ing
sud - den - ly ap - peared a fig - ure grey and

vi - sion of the ev - er - chang - ing
ghost - ly be - neath a flow - ing

view. A wond - 'rous wo - ven mag - ic in
beard. In times of deep - est dark - ness, I've

© 1971 (Renewed 1999) COLGEMS-EMI MUSIC INC.
All Rights Reserved International Copyright Secured Used by Permission

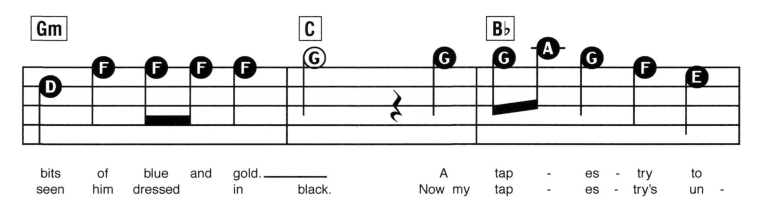

bits   of   blue and   gold._____   A   tap - es - try   to
seen him dressed in   black.   Now my tap - es - try's un -

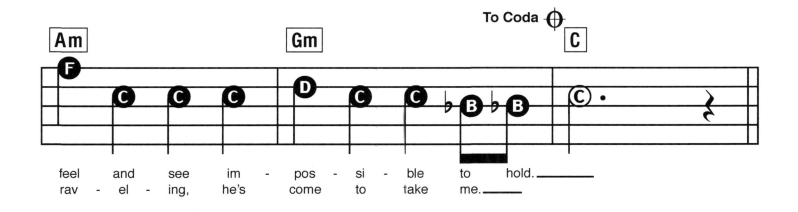

feel   and   see   im - pos - si - ble   to hold._____
rav - el - ing,   he's   come   to take me._____

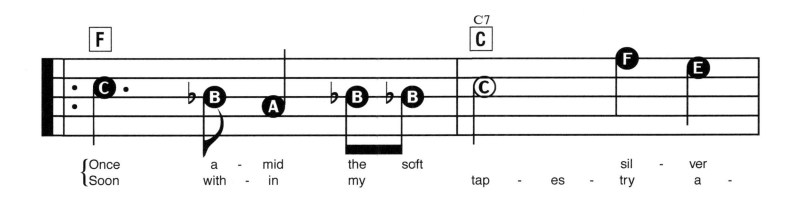

Once   a - mid   the soft   sil - ver
Soon   with - in   my   tap - es - try   a -

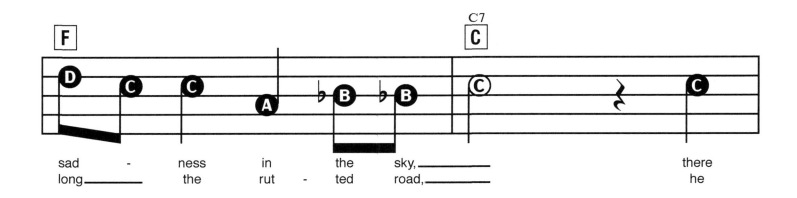

sad - ness in   the sky,_____   there
long_____ the   rut - ted road,_____   he

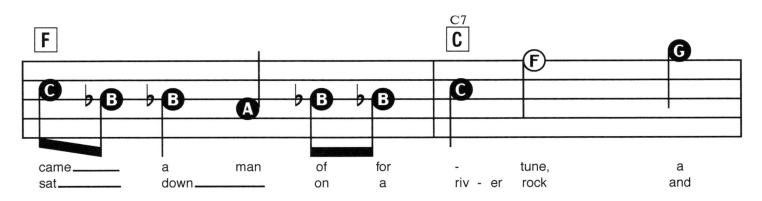

came_____ a man of for - tune, a
sat_____ down_____ on a riv - er rock and

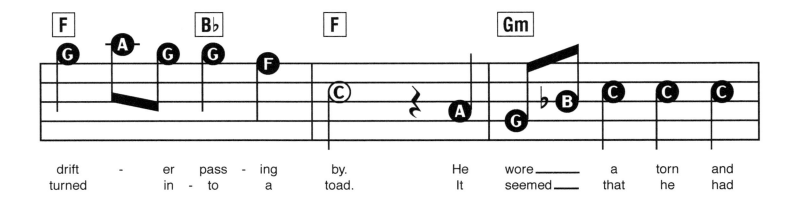

drift - er pass - ing by. He wore_____ a torn and
turned in - to a toad. It seemed_____ that he had

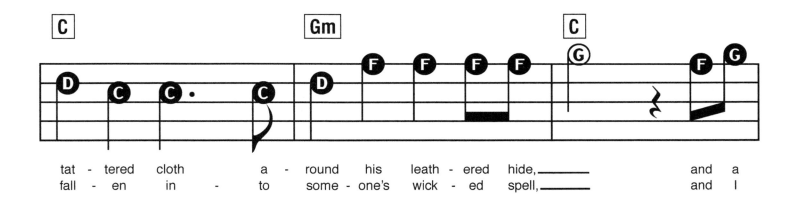

tat - tered cloth a - round his leath - ered hide,_____ and a
fall - en in - to some - one's wick - ed spell,_____ and I

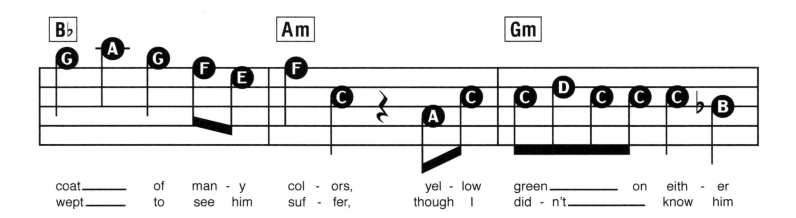

coat_____ of man - y col - ors, yel - low green_____ on eith - er
wept_____ to see him suf - fer, though I did - n't_____ know him

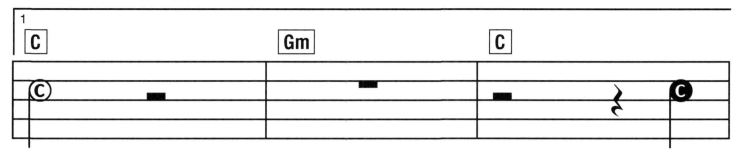

side.   He

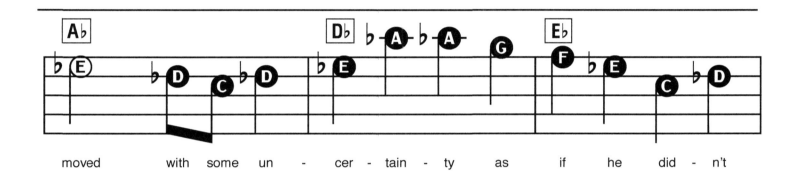

moved   with   some   un - cer - tain - ty   as   if   he   did - n't

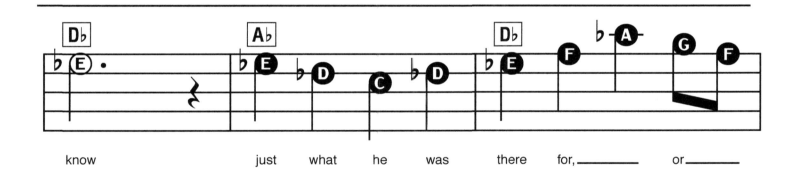

know   just   what   he   was   there   for,_____   or_____

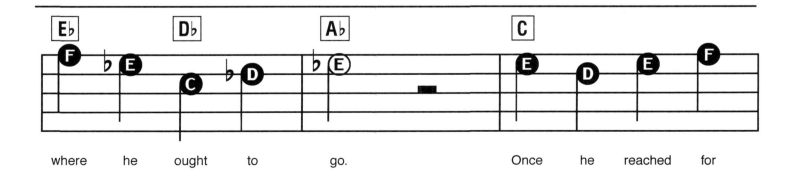

where   he   ought   to   go.   Once   he   reached   for

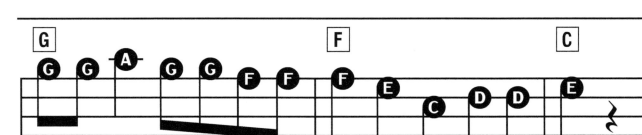

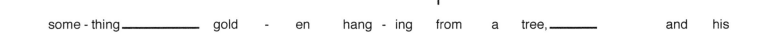

some - thing _____ gold - en hang - ing from a tree, _____ and his

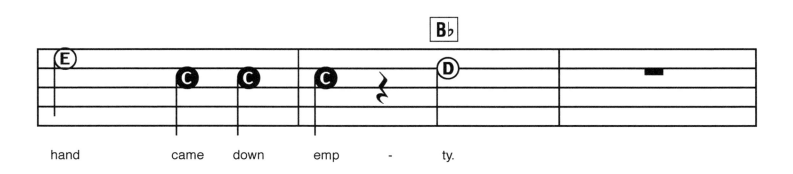

hand came down emp - ty.

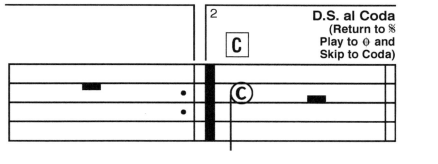

D.S. al Coda
(Return to %
Play to ⊕ and
Skip to Coda)

well.

CODA

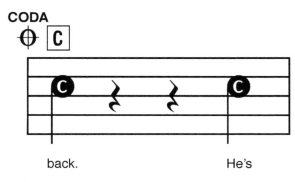

back. He's

C7

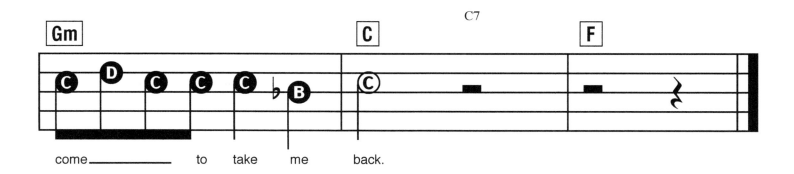

come _____ to take me back.

Up on the Roof

Registration 2
Rhythm: Ballad

Words and Music by Gerry Goffin
and Carole King

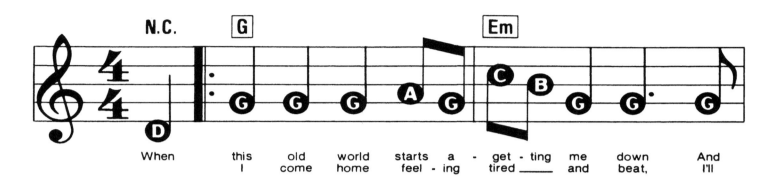

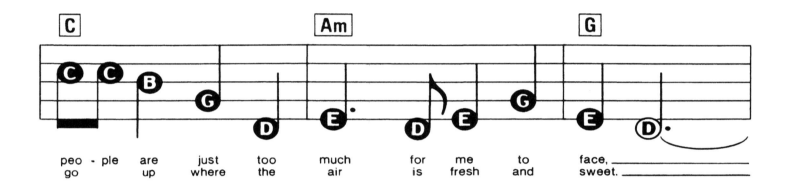

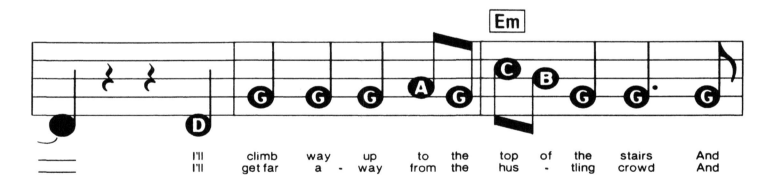

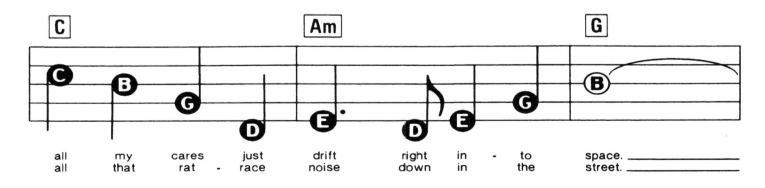

© 1962 (Renewed 1990) SCREEN GEMS-EMI MUSIC INC.
All Rights Reserved International Copyright Secured Used by Permission

On the roof it's peace - ful as can
On the roof that's the on - ly place I

be _____ And there the world be - low don't both - er
know _____ Where you just have to wish to make it

me. _____ So, when
so, _____ up on the

roof. At night the stars put on a show for

free _____ And, dar - ling, you can

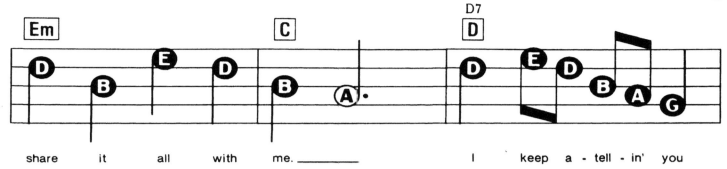

share it all with me. _____ I keep a - tell - in' you

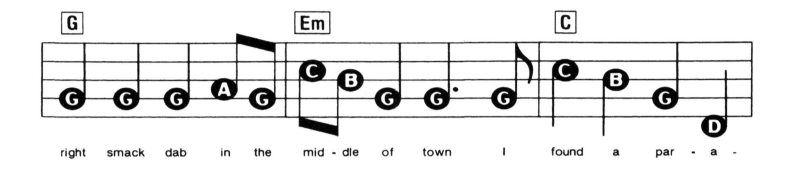

right smack dab in the mid - dle of town I found a par - a -

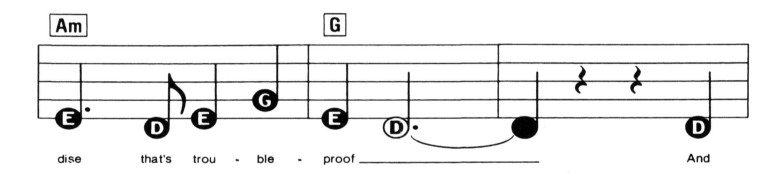

dise that's trou - ble - proof _____ And

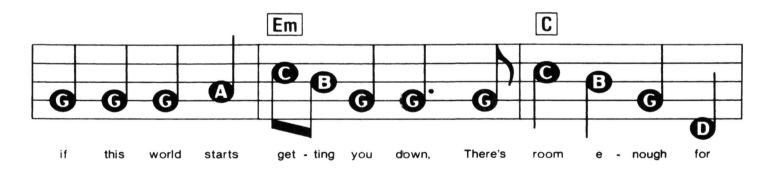

if this world starts get - ting you down, There's room e - nough for

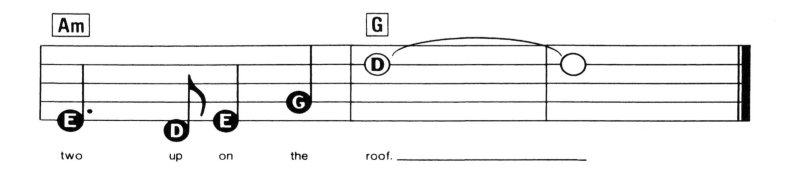

two up on the roof. _____

Where You Lead

Registration 4
Rhythm: 8-Beat or Rock

Words and Music by Carole King
and Toni Stern

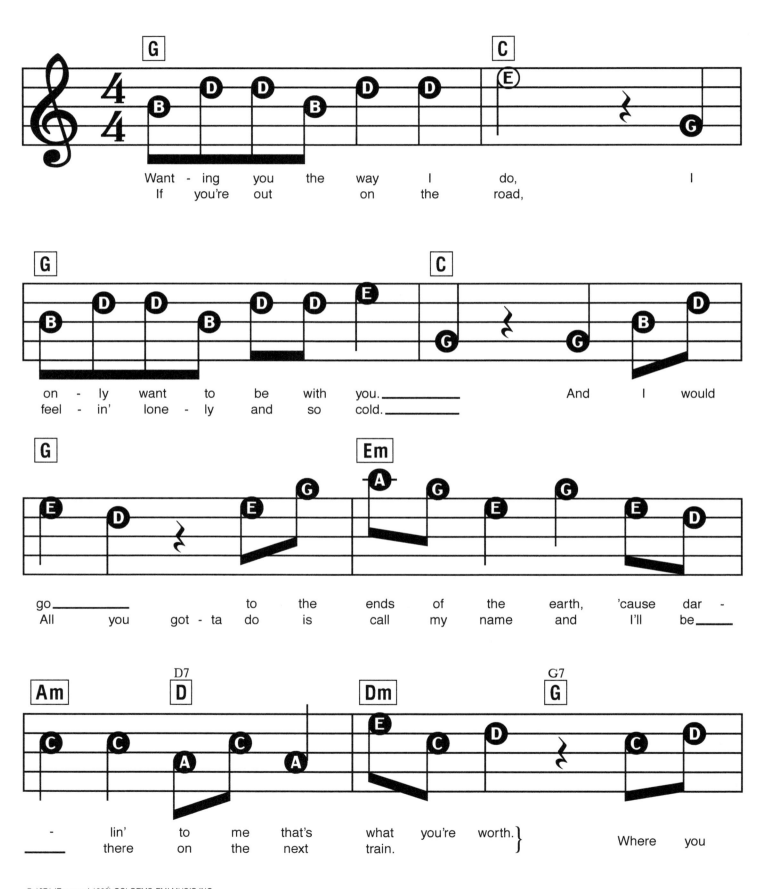

© 1971 (Renewed 1999) COLGEMS-EMI MUSIC INC.
All Rights Reserved   International Copyright Secured   Used by Permission

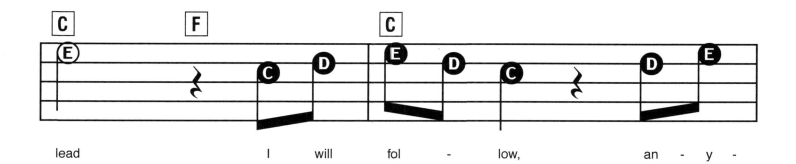

lead   I   will   fol - low,   an - y -

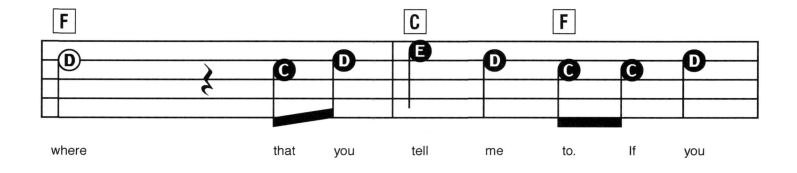

where   that   you   tell   me   to.   If   you

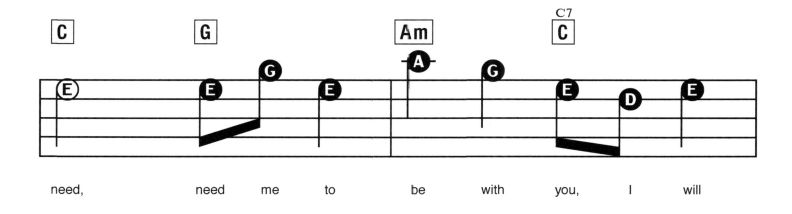

need,   need   me   to   be   with   you,   I   will

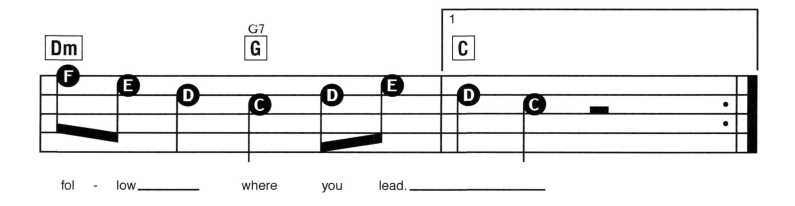

fol - low_____ where   you   lead._____

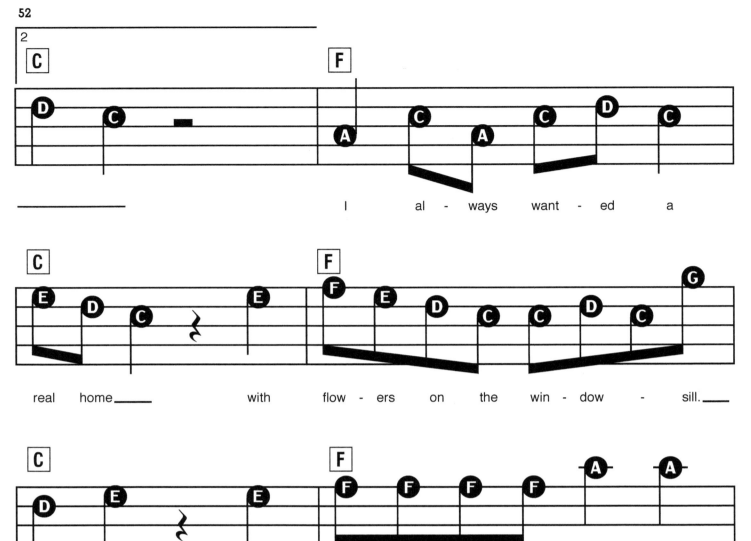

I al - ways want - ed a

real home_____ with flow - ers on the win - dow - sill.____

But, if you want to live in

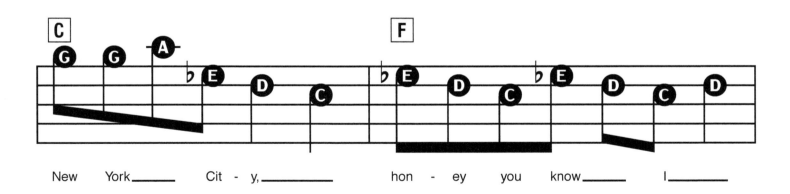

New York_____ Cit - y,_____ hon - ey you know_____ I_____

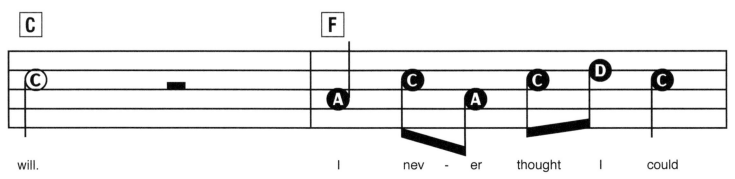

will. I nev - er thought I could

53

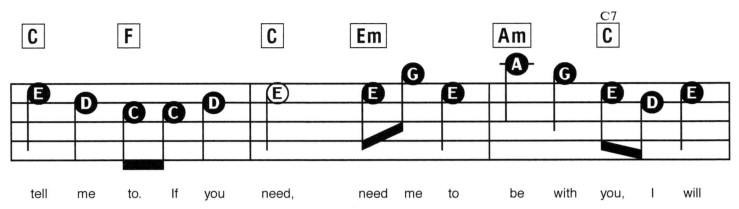

tell me to.   If you   need,   need me to   be   with   you,   I   will

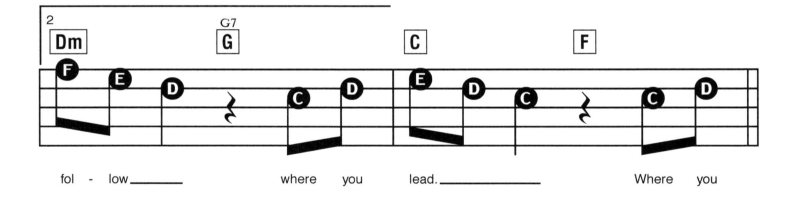

fol - low._____   Oh,_____   where   you_____

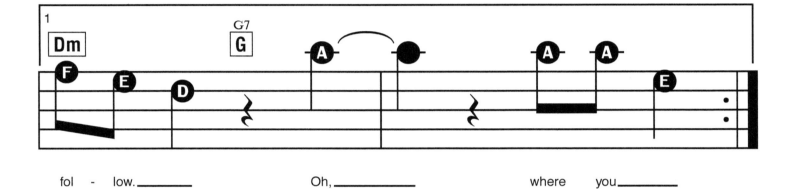

fol - low_____   where   you   lead._____   Where   you

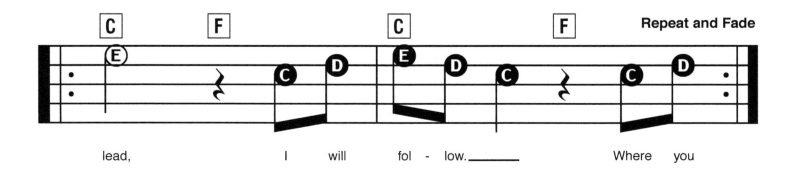

lead,   I   will   fol - low._____   Where   you

You've Got a Friend

Registration 3
Rhythm: Slow Rock or Ballad

Words and Music by
Carole King

© 1971 (Renewed 1999) COLGEMS-EMI MUSIC INC.
All Rights Reserved   International Copyright Secured   Used by Permission

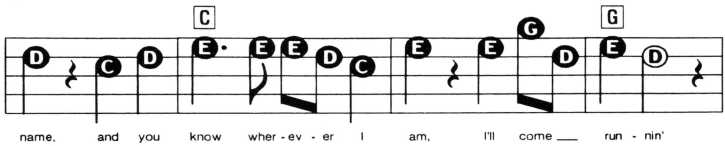

name, and you know wher-ev-er I am, I'll come ___ run-nin'

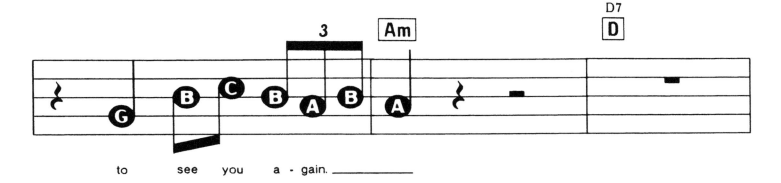

to see you a-gain. ___

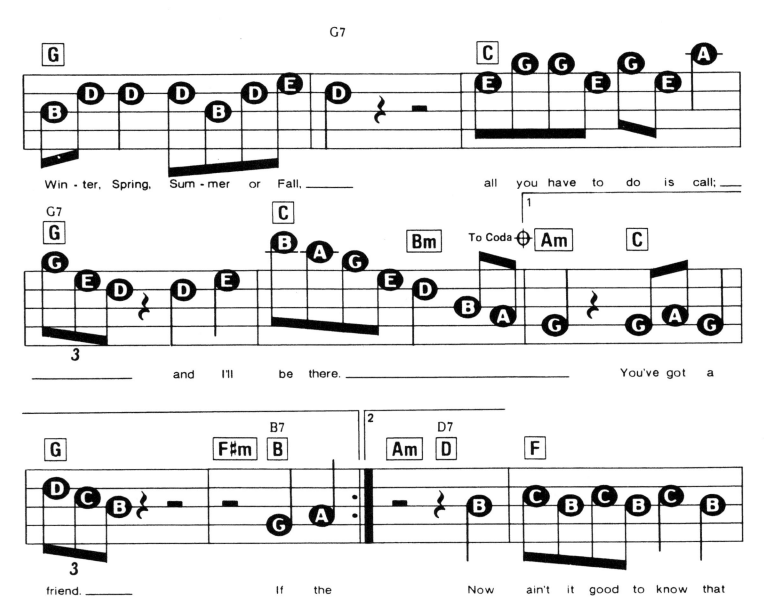

Win-ter, Spring, Sum-mer or Fall, ___ all you have to do is call; ___

___ and I'll be there. ___ You've got a

friend. ___ If the Now ain't it good to know that

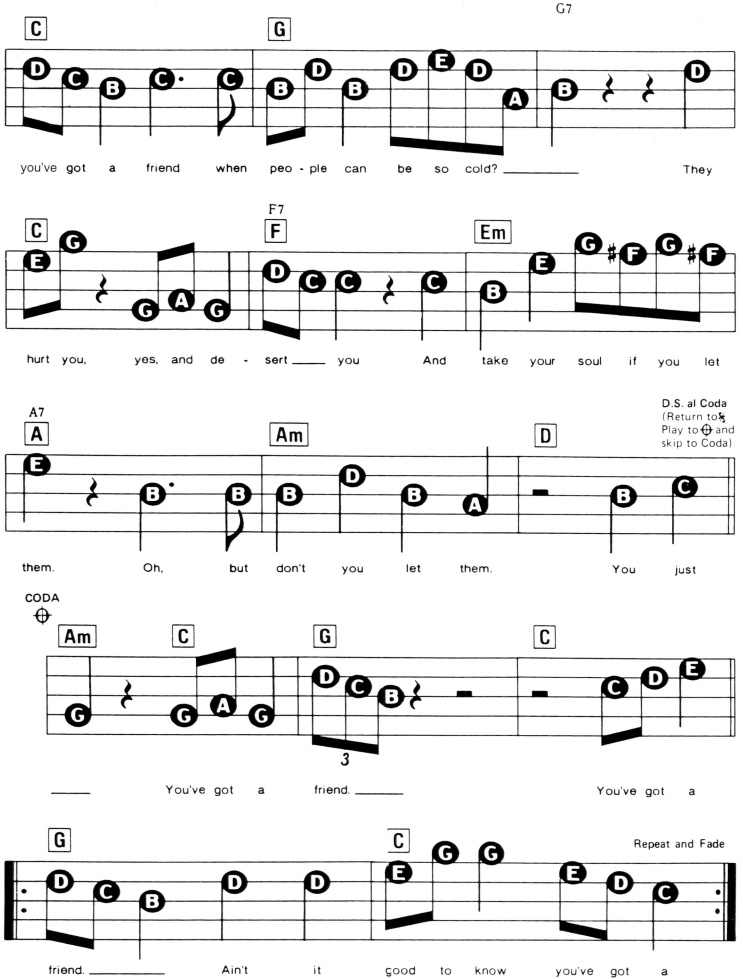

Will You Love Me Tomorrow
(Will You Still Love Me Tomorrow)

Registration 4
Rhythm: Rock

Words and Music by Gerry Goffin
and Carole King

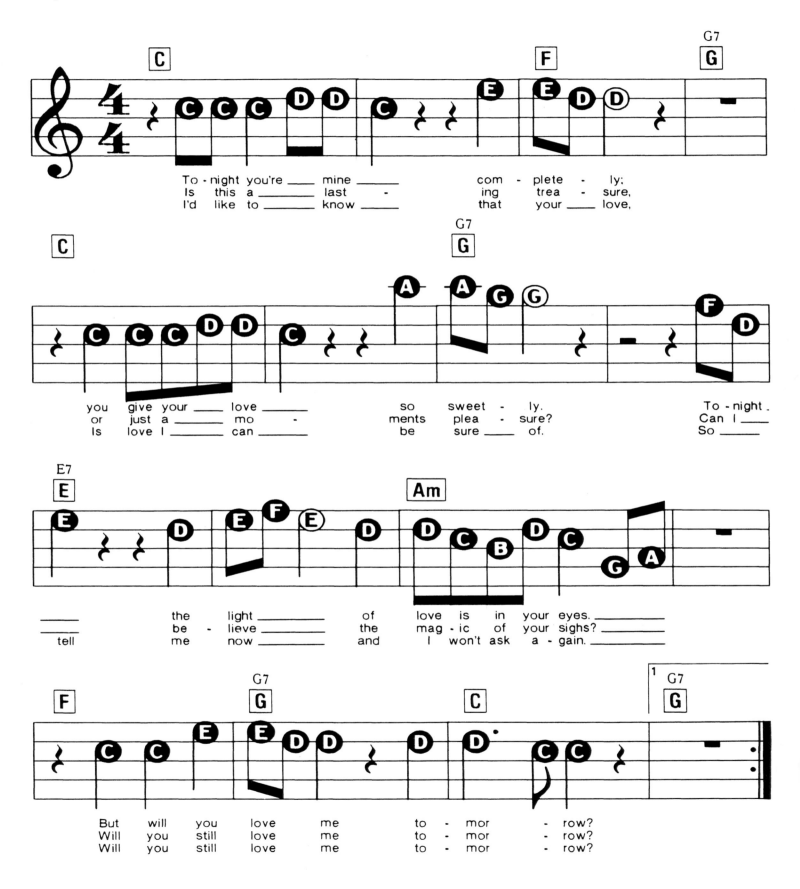

© 1961 (Renewed 1989) SCREEN GEMS-EMI MUSIC INC.
All Rights Reserved   International Copyright Secured   Used by Permission

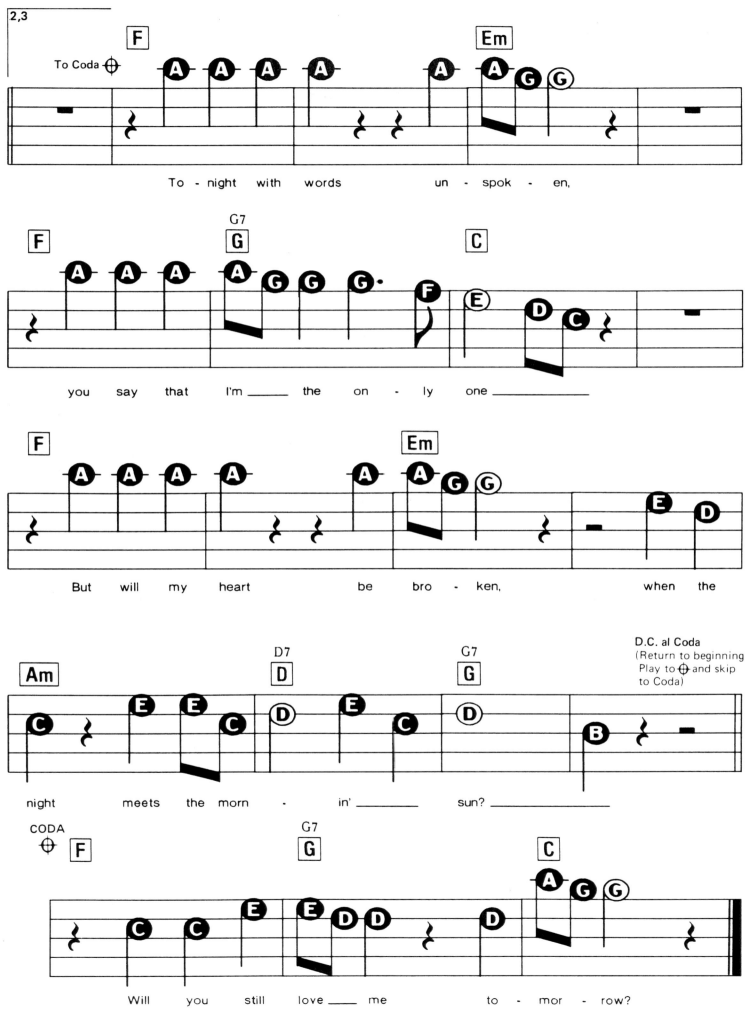

Registration Guide

- Match the Registration number on the song to the corresponding numbered category below. Select and activate an instrumental sound available on your instrument.

- Choose an automatic rhythm appropriate to the mood and style of the song. (Consult your Owner's Guide for proper operation of automatic rhythm features.)

- Adjust the tempo and volume controls to comfortable settings.

Registration

1	Mellow	Flutes, Clarinet, Oboe, Flugel Horn, Trombone, French Horn, Organ Flutes
2	Ensemble	Brass Section, Sax Section, Wind Ensemble, Full Organ, Theater Organ
3	Strings	Violin, Viola, Cello, Fiddle, String Ensemble, Pizzicato, Organ Strings
4	Guitars	Acoustic/Electric Guitars, Banjo, Mandolin, Dulcimer, Ukulele, Hawaiian Guitar
5	Mallets	Vibraphone, Marimba, Xylophone, Steel Drums, Bells, Celesta, Chimes
6	Liturgical	Pipe Organ, Hand Bells, Vocal Ensemble, Choir, Organ Flutes
7	Bright	Saxophones, Trumpet, Mute Trumpet, Synth Leads, Jazz/Gospel Organs
8	Piano	Piano, Electric Piano, Honky Tonk Piano, Harpsichord, Clavi
9	Novelty	Melodic Percussion, Wah Trumpet, Synth, Whistle, Kazoo, Perc. Organ
10	Bellows	Accordion, French Accordion, Mussette, Harmonica, Pump Organ, Bagpipes